What Is a
REFORMED
CHURCH?

Malcolm H. Watts

Foreword by Joel R. Beeke

Reformation Heritage Books
Grand Rapids, Michigan

What Is a Reformed Church?
© 2011 by Malcolm H. Watts

Reformation Heritage Books
2965 Leonard St. NE
Grand Rapids, MI 49525
616-977-0889
orders@heritagebooks.org
www.heritagebooks.org

Printed in the United States of America
18 19 20 21 22 23/11 10 9 8 7 6 5 4

Library of Congress Cataloging-in-Publication Data

Watts, Malcolm H.
  What is a reformed church? / Malcolm H. Watts ; foreword by Joel R. Beeke.
      p. cm.
  Includes bibliographical references and index.
  ISBN 978-1-60178-157-4 (pbk. : alk. paper) 1. Church—History of doctrines. 2. Reformed Church—Doctrines. I. Title.
  BV598.W38 2011
  262'.042—dc23
                         2011047562

For additional Reformed literature, request a free book list from Reformation Heritage Books at the above regular or e-mail address.

What Is a
REFORMED
CHURCH?

Contents

Foreword

Finally—a sound, concise, yet meaty little book on the basics of the Reformed faith, Reformed ecclesiology, and Reformed evangelism. *What Is a Reformed Church?* serves the church of Jesus Christ in several ways. Let me mention a few:

- It provides an *authoritative* treatment of the Reformed faith. "Thus saith the Lord" runs through every chapter. Substantial answers are offered to important questions; every page is packed with scriptural proof clarifying the mind of the Spirit as revealed in the Scriptures. God's will, not man's, is consulted in areas such as church government, church discipline, and church worship, areas where natural man is so eager to accommodate human tastes and wishes.

- It provides a *sound* treatment of the Reformed faith. For example, the author unabashedly upholds the regulative principle of Scripture for public worship. His book presents a well-reasoned and historically informed understanding of the Reformed perspective on worship, showing that God claims the right to determine the objects, occasions, forms, and content of our worship. He persuades us that worship must be viewed as a means of grace and must impact all that we are and do. Unlike so many contemporary works on worship by those who may even call themselves Reformed, the author refuses to allow carnal methods or content to infiltrate or compromise the worship of the church.

- It provides a *broad* treatment of the Reformed faith. The book does not fall into the trap of limiting Calvinism to five points. It also deals with God's kingdom rule, the covenant of grace, the experience of grace, the proclamation of the gospel, and the consecration of life.

- It provides a *balanced* treatment of the Reformed faith, stressing God's transcendence and sovereignty as well as man's depravity and responsibility. God's sovereignty in saving men and His offer of grace to sinners are both given their rightful due. Here is Reformed theology cogently, accurately, and simply presented.

- It provides an *experiential* treatment of the Reformed faith. The author underscores the necessity of the work of the Holy Spirit in the believer's heart and life. This book avoids the caricature of Calvinism as a harsh, cold system; rather, here is genuine, winsome Calvinism that, under the Spirit's tutelage, transforms hearts, minds, and lives.

- It provides a *tried* treatment of the Reformed faith. The author personally knows the faith. He has preached these truths in his own church and has implemented the biblical, godly way of worship that he promotes. I have watched him lead Reformed worship among his own people in a most biblical, edifying manner and have also had the privilege of preaching on several occasions to his dear flock, which has been well trained to listen to God's Word and to worship God with all their hearts.

- It provides a *doxological* treatment of the Reformed faith. This book's accent is on the humble and holy praise of an awe-inspiring, sovereign, personal God, who is worthy to be worshiped with all our mind, soul, and strength.

Malcolm Watts's *What Is a Reformed Church?* is an excellent work for those just discovering the Reformed faith as well as for those who are more advanced but need to be reminded of its distinctives. Ministers would do well to urge their consistories or sessions to provide a copy for every church member or family. Its biblical content, sanctified scholarship, challenging insights, and warm pastoral applications are just what the church needs today. I know of no better basic Reformed handbook for believers.

Read this book more than once. Discuss it with your friends. Let its truths penetrate your mind and souls. Bow and worship the sovereign God that it so ably presents.

Joel R. Beeke, President
Puritan Reformed Theological Seminary
Grand Rapids, Michigan

Acknowledgments

This book arose from a number of addresses given at a conference in Australia. These have now been edited and revised, although the preaching style has generally been retained in the interests of communication and clarity. I am very grateful to Alan and Rachel Finch, and also to Angela Magee, members of the church here in Salisbury, who have rendered very valuable assistance in preparing the material for publication. I would also like to thank all those at Reformation Heritage Books for their kind patience and great efficiency. And finally, I am most grateful to Dr. Joel R. Beeke, a highly esteemed and very dear friend, who first encouraged me to submit these pages for publishing and who has graciously written for the book such a supportive and generous foreword.

Malcolm H. Watts
Emmanuel Church
Salisbury, England

CHAPTER 1

The Distinctives of a Reformed Church

The church of the living God, the pillar and ground of the truth.

—1 Timothy 3:15

In our day, the term *Reformed* is used freely and without thought. Great variety exists among churches that claim this title. In many cases, the term means little more than some adherence to the "five points of Calvinism." The term has lost its great historical richness and depth as the struggles of the Reformation have faded into distant history. The stand taken by the Reformers is virtually forgotten, and many consider it irrelevant today. If, however, we have a true and earnest desire to maintain the faith and fight the adversaries of God's Word, we would do well to look back to those who so clearly searched the Scriptures and stood firmly for the great truths of the Word of God. This chapter will briefly examine the roots of the term *Reformed* and then highlight the distinctives of a Reformed church, namely biblical doctrine, pure worship, right government, spiritual discipline, and faithful evangelism.

If asked what a Reformed church is, one could give a short biblical answer from 1 Timothy 3:15: "the church of the living God, the pillar and ground of the truth." A true church, Reformed according to God's Word, is the dwelling place of

God, maintaining and declaring the truth which He has been pleased to reveal. However, over the course of the sixteenth and seventeenth centuries, the term *Reformed* was understood to have at least three quite specific meanings, so it will be helpful to take a brief look at the historic use of the term.

In the 1500s, people first used *Reformed* to refer to churches that, under the vigorous preaching of the early Reformers, separated from the corrupt Church of Rome. In 1517, Martin Luther nailed his Ninety-Five Theses to the door of the Castle Church in Wittenberg, Saxony. Writing shortly afterwards, in 1518, Luther called for reformation of the church. The pope issued a bull in 1520 condemning both Luther and his doctrines; but on receipt of that bull, Luther said, "For me, the die is cast. I despise alike Roman fury and Roman favor. I will not be reconciled or communicate with them."[1] As his teaching spread throughout Germany, churches abolished private masses, administered communion with bread *and* wine, and removed images from the buildings they used for the public worship of God. Churches that embraced Luther's doctrine soon became known as Reformed.

In the mid-1500s, the term assumed a new emphasis: It was used to identify the so-called Calvinist wing of the Reformation. Enthusiastic supporters of Luther became known as Lutherans, or even as "Adherents of the Augsburg Confession" (the first Reformation confession, drawn up by Melanchthon in 1530). But men like John Calvin (who preached in Geneva from 1536 to 1564) proceeded much further in reformation with respect to worship, government, and practice, and they

---

1. Roland H. Bainton, *Here I Stand: A Life of Martin Luther* (Oxford: Lion Publishing, 1978), 151.

came to be identified as "the Church Reformed according to the Word of God." This phrase was first used in article 6 of the Peace of Westphalia, a 1648 treaty intended to secure equal rights for Protestant churches within the boundaries of the Roman Empire.

The term *Reformed* evolved further until it came to identify churches that were Puritan in belief and in practice. The Puritan movement inherited Calvin's theological legacy but expanded his teaching on law, grace, and the covenants. Believing the visible church was still corrupted by the remains of popery, Puritans sought even more thorough reformation according to the Word of God. They pointed out that Reformed churches on the Continent already had abolished unbiblical forms, ceremonies, and vestments. They believed the English church was hardly deserving of the epithet *Reformed*; it was, they said, only "half-Reformed." Puritanism was responsible for a remarkable document, the Solemn League and Covenant, to which the Westminster Assembly, the general synod called by the Long Parliament for settling affairs in the Church of England, subscribed in 1643. The covenant committed to seek a "reformation of religion in the kingdoms of England and Ireland, in doctrine, worship, discipline and government, according to the Word of God and the example of the best reformed Churches."[2]

In all the cases considered above, we can see common distinctives between churches that have been called Reformed. It is true that, proceeding historically, the later Reformed churches were more consistent in the outworking of these

---

2. Westminster Assembly, The Solemn League and Covenant, in *Westminster Confession of Faith* (Glasgow: Free Presbyterian Publications, 1981), 359.

principles, yet it is clear that these emphases were present in each. Today, when the term is so loosely used, it is important to consider what these common distinctives were, and to understand that these essential attributes of a Reformed church are what make a biblical church.

Scripture Alone

A Reformed church must acknowledge Scripture, God's written Word, as the sole authoritative expression of the divine will for all aspects of church life. Luther recognized this, but it was Calvin who articulated it carefully. The Westminster theologians consistently followed through. At a council in Toulouse in 1229, the Church of Rome issued the following decree: "We prohibit also the permitting of the laity to have the books of the Old and New Testaments."[3] One dreadful consequence of this in the sixteenth century was that, apart from a few scattered copies of Wycliffe's translation, there were no English-language Bibles to be found in Britain. When Tyndale translated the New Testament and shipped numerous copies to England, Bishop Tunstall secured as many as he could find in order to burn them at St Paul's Cross, the northeast corner of the churchyard belonging to St. Paul's Cathedral. What a dreadful sight it must have been, to watch God's Word being publicly burned! The church and nation were without the Bible, and as a result, there was widespread ignorance, not only among the people, but also among the clergy. When John Hooper became bishop of Gloucester in 1551, he found that 168 of the 311 clergy in his diocese did not

---

3. William Cathcart, *The Papal System* (Philadelphia: American Baptist Publications Society,1872), 435.

know the Ten Commandments, and 31 of them did not know who first taught us the Lord's Prayer.[4] England was devoid of religious knowledge and understanding. Inevitably, the church became subject to the will and whim of men. All kinds of things were introduced without biblical warrant; error and corruption were allowed to spread unchecked.

The Reformers believed the Scriptures to be the pure Word of God. As Luther put it, they "ascribe[d] the entire Holy Scripture to the Holy Spirit."[5] At the famous Diet of Worms, he boldly declared, "Unless I am convinced by Scripture and plain reason—I do not accept the authority of popes and councils, for they have contradicted each other—my conscience is captive to the Word of God. I cannot and I will not recant anything, for to go against conscience is neither right nor safe. God help me."[6] As for Calvin, he too affirmed the total veracity of the Scriptures: "We owe to the Scripture the same reverence which we owe to God, because it has proceeded from Him alone, and it has nothing of man mixed with it."[7] In his *Institutes of the Christian Religion,* he insisted that the Scriptures constitute "the scepter of God,"[8] and he clearly demonstrated his belief that God's Word should order everything in His church.

For the Reformers, then, and also for the later Puritans, the Bible was infallible and inerrant. They consistently upheld its unique authority over the church's life and mission. The

---

4. J. C. Ryle, *Light from Old Times* (London: Thynne & Jarvis, 1924), 71.

5. John Warwick Montgomery, *God's Inerrant Word* (Minneapolis: Bethany Fellowship, 1974), 68.

6. Bainton, *Here I Stand*, 185.

7. Montgomery, *God's Inerrant Word*, 102.

8. John Calvin, prefatory address to King Francis, in *Institutes of the Christian Religion* (Philadelphia: Westminster Press, 1960), 1:12.

exhortation of William Tyndale was: "Without God's Word do nothing. And to his Word add nothing; neither pull anything there from.... Serve God as he hath appointed thee."[9] The Puritans sought consistently to apply this principle. Whatever lacked biblical authority they declared to be ungodly and unlawful, and they disowned human inventions and traditions. Accordingly, a church began to emerge that was truly Reformed according to the Word of God.

Israel's Pattern

The Puritans' purification of the church certainly was supported by Scripture. In the Jewish church of the Old Testament, God's Word was recognized as the one and only rule. In Deuteronomy 4:1–2, for example, we read the words of Moses: "Now therefore hearken, O Israel, unto the statutes and unto the judgments, which I teach you, for to do them, that ye may live, and go in and possess the land which the LORD God of your fathers giveth you. Ye shall not add unto the word which I command you, neither shall ye diminish ought from it, that ye may keep the commandments of the LORD your God which I command you."

In consequence, Jewish church life was regulated by the Word, by which standard controversies were settled and procedures established. Any deviation from Scripture's precise rule came under this solemn and fearful indictment: "their fear toward me is taught by the precept of men" (Isa. 29:13). The prophet summed it up well when he said, "To the law and to the testimony: if they speak not according to this word, it

---

9. William Tyndale, *Tyndale's Doctrinal Treatises* (Cambridge: Cambridge Univ. Press, 1848), 330.

is because there is no light in them" (Isa. 8:20). God's Word alone regulated Israel's belief and conduct, and warnings were given against any attempt to supplement the written Word. After stating that "every word of God is pure," Agar solemnly declared, "Add thou not unto his words, lest he reprove thee, and thou be found a liar" (Prov. 30:5–6).

Christ's Rule

The Lord Jesus Christ recognized Scripture's great authority. That is clear from the account we have of His temptations. Assailed three times by Satan, He met each insidious suggestion with the words, "It is written" (Matt. 4:4, 7, 10). Later, He charged Jewish leaders with disregarding God's Word, which they did by attaching importance to tradition (the oral law which the Jews pretended was handed down from Moses). "Why," He pointedly asked them, "do ye also transgress the commandment of God by your tradition?" (Matt. 15:3). Our Lord knew that the sacred rule of the written Word was above human precepts and practices. In the particular context of Matthew 15, He was chiefly concerned with matters relating to worship. He said, in effect, that if in our worship we follow the teaching and example of men, we take it upon ourselves to abrogate or annul the Word of God. "Thus have ye made the commandment of God of none effect by your tradition" (Matt. 15:6). And where does that leave us? Christ said of such people, "In vain they do worship me, teaching for doctrines the commandments of men" (v. 9). Christ's understanding was that true religion is founded on the Word of God. In worship, the only authority is such as can express itself by "Thus saith the Lord."

The Apostles' Foundation

Christ's apostles had the same conviction. They were careful to preach and teach from God's Word. In Acts 17:2, for example, we read of Paul that "as his manner was, [he] went in unto them, and three sabbath days reasoned with them out of the scriptures." He did not propound a philosophical theory. He did not present scientific proofs. He did not even appeal to Christian experience. What he did was to declare revealed and objective truth. He "reasoned with them out of the scriptures," and his hearers tested what they heard by recourse to that same source of authority. Later in the same chapter, we read that the Bereans "were more noble than those in Thessalonica, in that they received the word with all readiness of mind, and searched the scriptures daily, whether those things were so" (v. 11). In other words, their nobleness of mind was evinced by their investigation of the subject by the standard of Scripture. They insisted that the new message be judged at the bar of God's Word.

The apostolic epistles show that the early churches generally were willing to subject themselves to the written Word of God. So, we have the apostle Paul ordering the affairs of the Corinthian church by what he wrote under Christ's divine authority. The Corinthians were not to be a law to themselves, as though the authoritative Word somehow proceeded from their church (1 Cor. 14:36). Instead, they were to submit to the teaching of Paul's letter, which is summed up as "the commandments of the Lord" (v. 37). Similarly, we find Paul warning against "commandments of men, that turn from the truth" (Titus 1:14), and also of the inevitable result of such departure in "will worship" (Col. 2:23), forms of worship that proceed from human ingenuity, which chapter 3 will address in more detail.

In apostolic teaching, the Word of God is both authoritative and sufficient. Hence, we find this great statement in 2 Timothy 3:16–17: "All scripture is given by inspiration of God, and is profitable for doctrine, for reproof, for correction, for instruction in righteousness: that the man of God may be perfect, thoroughly furnished unto all good works."

The Church Today

A Reformed church recognizes the Bible's absolute authority over all its affairs. It does not acknowledge prelacy (hierarchical church government) as the source of authority; neither does it ascribe legislative power to a synod or council; such bodies have power only to apply and to obey what God has revealed in His Book. This is extremely important. The present state of evangelicalism shows there is great need to recognize that the Lord reigns through His Word (Ps. 110:2; Isa. 11:4). In His kingdom, or church, the worship, government, and practice must be according to His revealed will. No one has authority above Christ, and no one has authority alongside Him. He alone has the right to determine what will be done in His church. A Reformed church will recognize this. It will not go beyond the Word of the Lord.

God's Transcendence

A Reformed church emphasizes the divine sovereignty, majesty, and glory, and therefore the great gulf existing between God in His transcendence and man in his sin and misery.

The opening sentence of Calvin's *Institutes* reads, "Nearly all the wisdom we possess, that is to say, true and sound wisdom, consists of two parts: the knowledge of God and of ourselves."[10] What follows is recognition of God's incomprehensibility, which makes Him unknown to man unless somehow He decides to make Himself known. Calvin built his entire system of theology upon this perception of God as infinitely exalted, far beyond the reach of man. In an address to commemorate the four hundredth anniversary of Calvin's birth, Benjamin Warfield said: "It is *the vision of God and His Majesty*, in a word, which lies at the foundation of the entirety of Calvinistic thinking.... The Calvinist is the man who has seen God, and who, having seen God in His glory, is filled, on the one hand with a sense of his own unworthiness to stand in God's sight, as a creature, and much more as a sinner, and, on the other hand, with adoring wonder that nevertheless this God is a God who receives sinners."[11]

This was the distinctive doctrine of the Reformation. It was present in Luther's teaching, but it was even more prominent in Calvin's. Believing Scripture to be the ultimate source of all true knowledge of God, Calvin sought to ascertain exactly what Scripture revealed, and thus he drew aside the veil, as it were, to show us God in all the glory of His being. "Surely," he wrote, "his infinity ought to make us afraid to try to measure him by our own senses. Indeed, his spiritual nature forbids our imagining anything earthly or carnal of him. For the same reason, he quite often assigns himself a dwelling place in heaven."[12]

The Westminster divines, with astonishing precision of thought and language, articulated the truth that God really is

---

10. Calvin, *Institutes*, 1.1.1.

11. Benjamin B. Warfield, *Calvin as a Theologian and Calvinism Today* (Edinburgh: The Hope Trust, 1909), 15–16.

12. Calvin, *Institutes*, 1.13.1.

God. Consider this grand and awesome statement: "God hath all life, glory, goodness, blessedness, in and of himself; and is alone in and unto himself all-sufficient, not standing in need of any creatures which he hath made, not deriving any glory from them, but only manifesting his own glory, in, by, unto, and upon them: he is the alone foundation of being, of whom, through whom, and to whom, are all things; and hath most sovereign dominion over them, to do by them, for them, or upon them, whatsoever himself pleaseth."[13]

The Scriptures' Expression of God
The Bible lays powerful stress on the glory, majesty, and sovereignty of God. It confronts us with a God who, in His "otherness," surpasses all the thoughts and imaginations of human minds. God is higher than the highest, "the most high God" (Gen. 14:19). The Bible refers to Him as "the high and lofty One that inhabiteth eternity, whose name is Holy" (Isa. 57:15). Possessing in Himself all perfection, He has everything and needs nothing. He is the one self-sufficient and all-sufficient being. To cite Paul, "who hath first given to him, and it shall be recompensed unto him again? For of him, and through him, and to him, are all things: to whom be glory for ever. Amen" (Rom. 11:35–36). There can be none like Him in the heaven above or on the earth beneath. He has neither rival nor challenger; and vain is the attempt to find any who can come anywhere near to Him in glory. In His incomparable greatness, He Himself asks the question, "To whom then will ye liken me, or shall I be equal?" (Isa. 40:25). George Swinnock, the Puritan, rightly concluded, "To liken

---

13. Westminster Confession of Faith, II, 2.

God to any is the grossest idolatry, and to liken any to God is the grossest arrogancy."[14]

God's sovereignty is therefore absolute, extending to every detail of life and history. "He doeth according to his will in the army of heaven, and among the inhabitants of the earth: and none can stay his hand, or say unto him, What doest thou?" (Dan. 4:35). Indeed, as David once confessed, "For the kingdom is the LORD's: and he is the governor among the nations" (Ps. 22:28). God only is great. He wears a crown of supreme authority and almighty power. He is seated upon a throne of the highest dignity, ruling over this world, other worlds, and worlds unknown. All dominions are within His universal empire. Outside of His unchangeable and unfailing decree, nothing has ever happened, or can ever happen. Not even a sparrow, we are told, can fall to the ground without His permission and knowledge. What a God He is! His plans never fail; His actions can never be prevented. He is able to say, without fear of being contradicted, "Surely as I have thought, so shall it come to pass; and as I have purposed, so shall it stand" (Isa. 14:24); and again, "My counsel shall stand, and I will do all my pleasure" (46:10).

This is true in the sphere of His saving operations. "Salvation belongeth unto the LORD" (Ps. 3:8). He determines who will be saved, and it is He who makes sinners spiritually alive, removes their ignorance and prejudice, reveals Christ to them as Savior and Lord, imparts the precious grace of faith, and then receives them into full favor and fellowship with Himself. As the apostle Paul wrote, "For by grace are ye

---

14. George Swinnock, *Works of George Swinnock* (Edinburgh: James Nichol, 1868), 4:468.

saved through faith; and that not of yourselves: it is the gift of God: not of works, lest any man should boast" (Eph. 2:8–9). Surely we should bow before Him in humble submission, with contrite and humble hearts. The psalmist, after asking, "Who in the heaven can be compared unto the LORD? who among the sons of the mighty can be likened unto the LORD?," states that, in view of His infinite glory, "God is greatly to be feared in the assembly of the saints, and to be had in reverence of all them that are about him" (Ps. 89:6–7).

The Effect on Our Worship

In Reformed churches, the divine majesty is an article of faith, and it awakens godly fear in every act of public worship. There is orderliness in the services, and worshipers are aware that they are in the presence of Jehovah, the God of ineffable majesty. A biblical concept of God—what He is in Himself and what He is to His people—is fitted to inspire loftiest adoration and noblest praise. It certainly banishes light thoughts, flippant expressions, and worldly performances.

A very different atmosphere pervades the majority of modern churches. Even before the service begins, there is worldly and idle chatter. This breaks out again as soon as the service is over, effectively removing every good impression. Hearts do not appear to be devoted to the work of praise; there is careless inattentiveness to Scripture, and there is little intensity of devotion when it comes to prayer. Indeed, in not a few churches, music and group singing so dominates that the service becomes more like a concert. Tragically, there is this same ethos in some Reformed churches. Entering the building on the Sabbath day, one is confronted with styles and content of worship normally associated with modern,

Arminian, and charismatic churches. Reformed worship should be distinctive. We confess a sovereign God. Our veneration for Him should be demonstrated in the way we make our approach to Him. It should always be in a serious manner and with reverential fear.

The Way of Salvation

A Reformed church proclaims God's scheme of salvation, which is plainly set forth in the doctrines of free, sovereign, and distinguishing grace. In the late sixteenth and early seventeenth centuries, an important controversy took place in the Reformed churches of the Netherlands. Jacob Arminius (1560–1609), who had studied at Geneva, began to express views contrary to Scripture and the Reformed faith. As professor of theology at the University of Leyden, Arminius delivered a series of lectures on predestination, and many of the students who imbibed his novel and unorthodox views began to agitate for changes in the confession of faith and in the catechism. These men became known as the Remonstrants. In a document they called a "Remonstrance," they set forth their opinions under five heads:

1. God elected to save those who believe on the Son.

2. Jesus Christ, the Savior of the world, died for all men and every man.

3. Man needed to be born again of God in Christ. This, of course, was true enough.

4. The operation of divine grace is not irresistible.

5. According to some, those in Christ by a true faith may possibly become once again devoid of grace.

In 1618–1619, a General Synod was held at Dordrecht, with representatives (eighty-four in all) from the Netherlands, Great Britain, Germany, and Switzerland. The Synod began its sessions on November 13, 1618, and, after careful consideration of the Scripture, it dealt with the five articles of the Remonstrants, setting forth under five heads the true doctrine of God's Word:

1. Election is not based on foreseen faith but on God's good pleasure.

2. God, through the death of His Son, has effectually redeemed only those who from eternity were chosen to salvation.

3. and 4. Apart from regenerating grace, sinners are neither able nor willing to return to God, but all those in whom God works in this way are unfailingly regenerated and do actually believe.

5. Through undeserved mercy, believers are secure against the complete loss of faith and grace, and do not continue in backsliding so as finally to perish.

The Synod's five leading doctrines later became known as the five points of Calvinism. They are usually presented as follows.

Total Depravity

As a result of the Fall, people are totally alienated from God, subject to the corrupting power of sin, and in a totally helpless position: "dead in trespasses and sins" (Eph. 2:1). Such is the human state that people cannot will or do anything spiritual; they certainly cannot believe or repent. Christ said, "No man can come to me, except the Father which hath sent me draw him" (John 6:44), and early Jewish believers recognized that

"God [hath] also to the Gentiles granted repentance unto life" (Acts 11:18). This doctrine does not mean that people are as bad as they can possibly be. Rather, it means that we have been corrupted in the totality of our beings, so that every faculty has been impaired. Mind, heart, and will have all been adversely and tragically affected by sin. We are evidently therefore "without strength" (Rom. 5:6). As Paul made clear in Romans 9, this means that in the matter of salvation, "It is not of him that willeth, nor of him that runneth, but of God that sheweth mercy" (v. 16).

Unconditional Election

God's electing of a people is the eternal expression of His mercy and grace. God, who willed to permit the Fall, determined to rescue some from their sin and misery. Had He not done so, the whole human race would have perished under divine judgment like Sodom and Gomorrah (Rom. 9:29). It was therefore an election to salvation. That is exactly what Paul said in his letter to the Thessalonians: "We are bound to give thanks alway to God for you, brethren beloved of the Lord, because God hath from the beginning chosen you to salvation" (2 Thess. 2:13). This was according to God's own good pleasure, not according to anything foreseen in men and women. This is taught in passages of Scripture such as Ephesians 1:5. Elsewhere, the apostle categorically denied that God chooses sinners on the grounds of works foreseen. In Romans 9, for example, he said concerning Jacob and Esau that "the children being not yet born, neither having done any good or evil," God showed His sovereign preference for Jacob in order that "the purpose of God according to election might stand" (v. 11).

Election is gracious. It is never deserved. God did not foresee that certain individuals would repent and believe, and then upon that basis, elect them to eternal life. That would make His choice dependent upon merit, whereas election is by God's free favor: "Even so then at this present time also there is a remnant according to the election of grace. And if by grace, then it is no more of works: otherwise grace is no more grace" (Rom. 11:5–6). In His eternal decree, God viewed mankind as fallen and ruined. He determined, in His own mind, to show mercy to multitudes, while justly leaving others to the consequences of the Fall. Instead of questioning this doctrine, we should fall before the throne in praise and thanksgiving, for if God had not elected some, every single soul would face a dark and fearful eternity. As it is, multitudes upon multitudes will be in the kingdom of heaven, to the glory of sovereign grace!

Limited Atonement

This point, sometimes called *particular atonement*, teaches that the Son redeemed those elected by the Father. In other words, Christ did not die for everyone, but only for the chosen people of God. Christ's own statement was "the good shepherd giveth his life for the sheep" (John 10:11; see also v. 15). He would never have said that He gives His life for the goats. In Acts 20:28, Paul told the Ephesian elders to look after God's church, "which he hath purchased with his own blood." So, what has been bought? What now is the Lord's special possession: the whole human race, or the chosen part of it? The answer to all these questions is—the church!

We are told that the glorified in heaven sing this new song: "Thou art worthy to take the book, and to open the seals thereof: for thou wast slain, and hast redeemed us to God by thy blood out of every kindred, and tongue, and people, and nation" (Rev. 5:9). Let me state the obvious. They are not singing that He redeemed every kindred, tongue, people, and nation, but that he redeemed *us* out of every kindred, tongue, people, and nation. Christ died to save the elect. His was *particular* redemption.

Effectual Calling

Since by reason of sin we have lost the ability to will and do any spiritual good, we cannot even answer the call of mercy in the gospel. God therefore calls us not only by His Word, but also by His Spirit, who powerfully draws us to Christ that we might be saved. "No man can come to me," Jesus said, "except the Father which hath sent me draw him" (John 6:44). As Paul was careful to explain, "There is one body, and one Spirit, even as ye are called in one hope of your calling" (Eph. 4:4).

Is the Spirit's work always effectual? Yes, it certainly is. There is a great verse in Romans which says, "Moreover whom he did predestinate, them he also called: and whom he called, them he also justified: and whom he justified, them he also glorified" (8:30). Who, then, are the "called"? Are they all those people who hear the gospel of Christ? No! Looking back, they are those who were predestinated; and looking forward, they are those who will be justified, and ultimately glorified. This calling, peculiar to the elect, is God's way of saving people in time and for eternity. Accordingly, we find that to be *called* (in this sense) is nothing more nor less than to be *saved*. The words are used interchangeably, as in 1 Corinthians 1, where the gospel is said, on the one hand, to be "the power of God" to the "saved," and on the other hand, "the power of God" to the "called" (vv. 18, 24). The calling is viewed as all one with being brought into a state of salvation, and so the apostle can write in another place: "[God] hath saved us, and called us with an holy calling" (2 Tim. 1:9). How indebted we all are to this sovereign and irresistible call, which does not simply invite, but graciously brings us to Christ!

John Bunyan's *The Pilgrim's Progress* contains a helpful little illustration. In the Interpreter's House, Christiana encounters a hen and its chicks. The Interpreter points out that the hen "had a *common* call, and that she hath all day long"; but he goes on to say that she also "had a *special* call, and that she had but sometimes" (italics added). We have all observed a mother hen clucking in such a way that her chicks come running to her. This shows us the different ways in which the Lord deals with men and women. When He calls in a general way in the gospel, sinners will not come to Him, but when He calls them effectually by His Spirit, they come running, to find their refuge under the shadow of His wings. As Bunyan's Interpreter says, "by his common call he gives nothing," whereas "by his special call, he always has something to give."[15]

Perseverance of the Saints

True believers will never totally or finally fall away. They will continue in faith and holiness to the end of their lives. "The righteous also shall hold on his way, and he that hath clean hands shall be stronger and stronger" (Job 17:9). This is not because of anything in them. Rather, it is because God will carry on the work of grace to completion: "He which hath begun a good work in you will perform it until the day of

---

15. John Bunyan, *The Pilgrim's Progress*, in *Works* (Glasgow: Blackie & Son, 1854), 3:186.

Jesus Christ" (Phil. 1:6). God has no intention of abandoning His people, nor of forsaking the work of His hands. "The author" of their faith will also be its "finisher" (Heb. 12:2). Why? Because "the gifts and calling of God are without repentance" (Rom. 11:29). God does not bestow grace for a temporary purpose. He will never withdraw it and leave a soul to perish. Believers are therefore eternally safe and secure. Christ said, "I give unto them eternal life; and they shall never perish, neither shall any man pluck them out of my hand" (John 10:28).

God's Covenant of Grace

A Reformed church understands that a covenant is at the heart of God's relationship with man. Therefore, Reformed churches emphasize the unfolding and developing of God's covenant of grace. John Murray called covenant theology "a distinguishing feature of the reformed tradition."[16]

Biblically speaking, a covenant is an arrangement into which God enters for the benefit of men and women. The Reformers recognized the importance of this concept, and made free use of it in their sermons and writings. The doctrine of the covenant is found seminally in Calvin's *Institutes,* but those who came after him developed it. In 1561, Zacharius Ursinus, a professor at Heidelberg, referred to a covenant God made with Adam before the Fall, and in 1576, Ursinus's colleague Caspar Olevianus taught that there was another covenant which was fulfilled in Christ to the everlasting salvation of God's elect people.

---

16. John Murray, *Collected Writings of John Murray* (Edinburgh: Banner of Truth, 1982), 4:216.

The Covenants of Works and Grace

There are two covenants that relate to eternal life. They are usually referred to as the *covenant of works* and the *covenant of grace*, the former being that bond established with Adam, the representative of mankind, and the latter being the bond established from eternity with the Son of God, the representative and surety of God's elect.

God entered into the covenant of works with Adam soon after his creation (Gen. 2:16–17; see also Hos. 6:7 margin). The *condition* of this covenant was Adam's personal and perfect obedience—that is, his works. This obedience was tested by the command not to eat the fruit of the tree of knowledge of good and evil. But alongside the condition was the *penalty* of death, which included physical, spiritual, and eternal death (Rom. 5:12; 6:23); by implication, there was the *promise* of life, in the same three forms and culminating in eternal life (Matt. 19:16–17; Rom. 7:10). We know that Adam, by sinning, breached that covenant, plunging himself and all his posterity into ruin: "As by one man sin entered into the world, and death by sin; and so death passed upon all men, for that [or, in whom] all have sinned" (Rom. 5:12).

In His great kindness, God revealed, almost at once, the existence of another covenant: the covenant of grace. He had made this arrangement in eternity with the Son of God (Gal. 3:17; Eph. 3:11), who was then appointed "the last Adam" or "the second [representative] man" (1 Cor. 15:45, 47). Its condition was also obedience, but this was to be not just active obedience in life; it was also to be passive obedience in suffering and death, to answer for the sin of the broken covenant. Hence, the Son was obliged to "fulfil all righteousness" (Matt. 3:15). He had to be "obedient unto death" (Phil. 2:8). That the condition would be met was never in doubt, so no penalty was associated with this covenant. God declared that He would honor the promise, and bestow the gift of eternal life to His incarnate Son and to every one of His people (Titus 1:2; 1 John 5:11). In the fullness of time, Christ—the mediator of the new covenant—succeeded where Adam had miserably failed. He could say, "I restored that which I took not away" (Ps. 69:4).

When, by faith, sinners unite with Christ, their head and representative, they are incorporated into this saving covenant and obtain its blessing for time and eternity. "For God so loved the world, that he gave his only begotten Son, that whosoever believeth in him should not perish, but have everlasting life" (John 3:16). The divine purpose in giving us the Scriptures is to reveal this glorious covenant of grace, in various typical covenants (see, for example, Gen. 9:8–17; 17:1–14; Ex. 24:1–8) and supremely in the gospel of Christ (Isa. 55:3; Luke 1:68–72; Heb. 10:15–25). How this doctrine magnifies divine grace! God was not obliged to have dealings with man, or to bless him in any way whatsoever, and yet in His amazing grace He made an arrangement in Christ which issues in a life of eternal blessedness.

Edward Payson, the American Congregational minister, wrote to his mother in 1812. He had been thinking privately about the wonders of God's grace, and in this particular letter, he expressed some profound thoughts on that subject. He wrote:

> Never before did the scheme of redemption, and the great mystery of God manifest in the flesh, appear so great and glorious. While meditating upon it, I was wonderfully struck with a reason, which never occurred to me before, why God permitted Adam to fall. Had he stood, all his posterity would have been happy. He would, therefore,

in one sense, have been their Saviour; and while they were enjoying the happiness of heaven, they would have exclaimed, "For all this we are indebted to our first parent." This would have been too great an honour for any finite being. It would have tempted Adam to pride, and us to idolatry. The honour, therefore, was reserved for God's own Son, the second Adam. But perhaps this has occurred to you before; so I will not enlarge.[17]

Covenant theology exalts the glory of the Redeemer. It teaches the necessity of faith—that is, union with Him. For while we have a natural union with Adam, who brought us ruin and despair, we need a spiritual union with Christ, which will bring us life forevermore. If through faith we are one with Christ, everything He has is made over to us. And this includes, of course, His great salvation. Amazing though it is, spiritual paupers and debtors are now made the beneficiaries of rich, free grace and inheritors of a heavenly and everlasting kingdom.

An Experience of Grace

A Reformed church stresses the need for an inward, spiritual experience of God's saving grace, which creates such gratitude that believers readily follow the law as the rule of life. Luther entered an Augustinian monastery determined to live under the rules that regulated the whole of his life. Why did he become a monk? In his own heart, he felt the need for peace and hope. As he would later say, "If ever a monk could win heaven by monkery, I must have reached it."[18] Dr. Staupitz, the

---

17. Edward Payson, *A Memoir of the Rev. Edward Payson* (London: Seeley & Burnside, 1830), 235–36.

18. Thomas M. Lindsay, *Luther and the German Reformation* (Edinburgh, T. & T. Clark, 1908), 34.

prior of the Augustinians, insisted that every monk read the Scriptures. Luther began to study the epistle to the Romans. Later, he told movingly of his conversion to Christ:

> I sought day and night to make out the meaning of Paul, and at last I came to apprehend it thus: through the gospel is revealed the righteousness which availeth with God—a righteousness by which God, in his mercy and compassion, justifieth us; as it is written, "The just shall live by faith." Straightway I felt as if I were born anew. It was as if I had found the door of Paradise thrown wide open. Now I saw the Scriptures altogether in a new light.... The expression, "the righteousness of God," which I so much hated before, now became dear and precious—my darling and comforting word. That passage of Paul was to me the true door of Paradise.[19]

That is Reformed experience. It is something that is known and felt. Today, I fear, there is a great deal of intellectual Calvinism. Many people have book learning and head knowledge. But Reformed Christianity emphasizes the need to be inwardly taught. It emphasizes the things of the heart. It is possible for a mere professor of faith to know the doctrines of grace. The vital thing is to know "the grace of God in truth" (Col. 1:6; see also Eph. 1:13). True believers know something of Christ's love-visits (John 14:23; 16:22), times when He seems particularly near. His presence then stirs our graces, and our hearts thrill at the sound of His voice. We begin to feel the gracious influences of His Spirit. In those precious moments, the secrets of love are shared in real communion. This is heaven upon earth.

---

19. Lindsay, *Luther and the Reformation*, 36–37.

Now, *felt* grace does not destroy a believer's obligation to keep the law; rather, it strengthens that obligation, supplying new motives, abilities, and encouragements. The great English Puritan Richard Sibbes once observed that Christ's love "hath a constraining, a sweet violence to put us upon all duties, to suffer, to do, to resist anything."[20] Through the blessed ministry of the Holy Spirit, the believer's heart is inclined and drawn forth to obey God's holy laws. The promise is, "I will put my laws into their mind, and write them in their hearts" (Heb. 8:10), and the fulfilment is in that change which enables a sinner to say, "I delight in the law of God after the inward man" (Rom. 7:22).

So, is the law a rule of life for believers? Undoubtedly it is! The apostle was able to describe himself as "not without law to God, but under the law to Christ" (1 Cor. 9:21). In other words, as one of Christ's redeemed sinners, Paul felt himself indispensably bound to the moral law of God. Reformed believers regard the law neither as a means of justification nor as a means of condemnation. It is simply the rule of their duty.

Proclamation of the Gospel

A Reformed church is committed to the work of bringing the gospel of salvation to the unconverted, not only in its own vicinity but also in other areas of the country and in other parts of the world. Historically, reformation and evangelism have gone hand in hand.

In 1559, Protestants in Sweden took the gospel to the people of Lapland, and in 1562, French Protestants evangelized

---

20. Richard Sibbes, *The Works of Richard Sibbes* (Edinburgh: James Nichol, 1862), 2:74.

Florida and, afterwards, Carolina. In 1566, the church in Geneva sent fourteen missionaries to spread the Christian faith in South America. Later, the Pilgrim Fathers became missionaries. Arriving at New Plymouth, Massachusetts, in 1620, they soon organized a mission to promote the conversion of the Indians.

It is the duty of the church to evangelize. Among Christ's last words to His disciples were those recorded in Matthew's gospel: "Go ye therefore, and teach [or, make disciples of] all nations" (Matt. 28:19; see also v. 20; Mark 16:15–16; Luke 24:46–49; John 20:21–22). The book of Acts describes how His Great Commission was fulfilled. His believing people took the gospel from Jerusalem to other parts of Judea, then into regions inhabited by the Samaritans, and finally out to the very ends of the earth. This matter is no side issue. It is our great work to tell out the glories of God as they are displayed in the grand scheme of redemption. Why? Because only in this way will the divine purpose be fulfilled and "the earth…be filled with the knowledge of the glory of the LORD, as the waters cover the sea" (Hab. 2:14; see also Isa. 11:9). Preaching only in chapel buildings cannot realize this great vision. Christ's way is to "send forth labourers" (Matt. 9:38; see also John 15:16). As the apostle Paul said, "the word of the Lord" must have "free course," speeding its way throughout the whole world, if it is to be "glorified" in the revelation of its glorious truths and in the performing of its glorious works (2 Thess. 3:1).

Consecration of Life

A Reformed church will encourage the spirit of true devotion, which will find expression in lives wholly consecrated to God. Calvin's emblem was a hand holding out a heart to God, and his motto was, "I offer my heart to God as a sacrifice." Writing of the Christian life, Calvin remarked, "We are not our own, we belong to the Lord. We are not our own. Let our reasons and our wills then never predominate in our thinking and in our acting.... Let us then forget ourselves as much as is possible."[21]

That is the spirit of the Reformation. Those possessing it are willing to be mastered by God. What does the New Testament say? "For whether we live, we live unto the Lord; and whether we die, we die unto the Lord: whether we live therefore, or die, we are the Lord's" (Rom. 14:8). In another epistle, we read, "Ye are not your own.... Ye are bought with a price: therefore glorify God in your body, and in your spirit, which are God's" (1 Cor. 6:19–20). If a church is really biblical and Reformed, its members will be fully committed to Christ. The time has come for self-examination. Do we sincerely love the Lord? What kind of service do we offer Him? My friends, could it be that we are Reformed in name only?

---

21. Jean Cadier, *The Man God Mastered* (London: Inter-Varsity Fellowship, 1960), 105.

CHAPTER 2

The Great Emphasis of Reformed Doctrine

The blessed and only Potentate, the King of kings and Lord of lords.

—1 Timothy 6:15

More than any other, God's sovereignty is the doctrine most closely linked to the Reformed church. This is not surprising, as the leading Reformers had a deep understanding of sovereignty. Calvin gave a masterly treatment of it in his *Institutes*. Today, many speak of the sovereignty of God, but few have the biblical depth of understanding that Calvin and the other Reformers had, and few see the implications of it in their Christian lives.

This chapter will explore what the Bible teaches about the nature of God's sovereignty and how it is displayed, especially in salvation. We will then consider how Christians ought to respond to this great Reformation doctrine.

Unlimited Power and Might

Scripture teaches that God is God, which means that He has unlimited power and might to maintain supreme dominion over all creation. Deuteronomy 4:39 reads, "The LORD he is God." A weak deity is an absurdity. Power—highest power— must come into any adequate idea of God. Remember God's own words to Abram: "I am the Almighty God; walk before me, and be thou perfect" (Gen. 17:1). This "almightiness" is necessitated by the very nature of His being. A perfect being cannot have any deficiency; God must have power in infinite perfection. Mention is therefore made of "the exceeding greatness of his power" and of the fact that God is "able to do exceeding abundantly above all that we ask or think" (Eph. 1:19; 3:20). We call the exercise of this divine power *sovereignty.* God sovereignly determines the working of His omnipotence. As the psalmist says, "But our God is in the heavens: he hath done whatsoever he hath pleased" (Ps. 115:3; see also 135:6).

We should distinguish between the "absolute" and the "actual" power of God. By the former, we mean the power by which He is able to do anything (that is, anything consistent with the perfection of His nature). By the latter, we mean the power that, according to the determination of His will, He actually exerts in this world and in all other worlds. Nothing is impossible with God. He Himself says, "Behold, I am the LORD, the God of all flesh: is there any thing too hard for me?" (Jer. 32:27). But He has chosen to manifest His power in performing certain works, saying, "My counsel shall stand, and I will do all my pleasure" (Isa. 46:10).

John the Baptist said that "God is able of these stones to raise up children unto Abraham" (Matt. 3:9), but that is a far cry from saying that He has actually willed to do such a thing. Similarly, in the Garden of Gethsemane, our Lord said, "Thinkest thou that I cannot now pray to my Father, and he shall presently give me more than twelve legions of angels?" (Matt. 26:53). That was indeed within the divine power, but it was not something God saw fit to do. God's sovereignty is His ordering of all things according to His own predetermined and all-embracing purpose. It is in His sovereignty that God rules the whole created universe. The words of David come to mind, although many other scriptures could be quoted at this point. David said, "Thine, O LORD, is the greatness, and the power, and the glory, and the victory, and the majesty: for all that is in the heaven and in the earth is thine; thine is the kingdom, O LORD, and thou art exalted as head above all" (1 Chron. 29:11).

Infinite Superiority

God's unbounded sovereignty is founded on the infinite superiority of His nature. As the one who excels in greatness and goodness (as revealed in creation, providence, and redemption), He has lawful dominion over the entire creation. In the seventeenth century, the British Baptist preacher Benjamin Keach published a catechism based on the Westminster Shorter Catechism. I have always been impressed with its first question: "Who is the first and best of beings?" The answer, of course, is "God is the first and best of beings."[1]

Because God is the first being, "from everlasting to everlasting" (Ps. 90:2), and the best being, described as altogether "perfect" (Matt. 5:48), He has an unassailable right to reign over everything. As the cause of creation, He possesses authority to do what He pleases with His own property. "Is it not lawful for me to do what I will with mine own?" (Matt. 20:15; see also Rom. 9:20–21). And, as the *end* of creation, He has authority to order objects and events to show forth His

---

1. Baptist General Assembly, "*The London Baptist Confession of Faith of 1689 & Keach's Catechism*" (Choteau, Mont.: Gospel Mission, 1990), 1.

excellence and to secure great honor and glory. The very reason the worlds were made was to display the divine grandeur, greatness, and goodness. That is why God chooses to direct all creatures and events. It is to secure His everlasting praise. Scripture says, "For of him, and through him, and to him, are all things: to whom be glory for ever. Amen" (Rom. 11:36).

Freedom from Obligation

In His sovereignty, God is free from all influences, obligations, and motives outside of Himself. He does exactly what He pleases. What do we read? "He doeth according to his will in the army of heaven, and among the inhabitants of the earth: and none can stay his hand, or say unto him, What doest thou?" (Dan. 4:35); and again, "[He] worketh all things after the counsel of his own will" (Eph. 1:11). God's will is never frustrated, neither by the hostility of Satan nor by the rebellion of men. Psalm 33:11 reads, "The counsel of the LORD standeth for ever, the thoughts of his heart to all generations." God does have a will of purpose in all His works of creation, providence, and redemption, and it is pointless to challenge that will, for as Job said, "what his soul desireth, even that he doeth" (Job 23:13). This might profitably be compared to Proverbs 21:30: "There is no wisdom nor understanding nor counsel against the LORD."

It should be remembered, however, that God's eternal will is a secret. Generally speaking, He does not make it known or explain the reason for His works; "he giveth not account of any of his matters" (Job 33:13). Sometimes, however, He does inform others of His purpose, as in the case of Abraham, about whom God said, "Shall I hide from Abraham that thing which I do?" (Gen. 18:17; see also Amos 3:7). Since men are not initiated into all the divine counsels, it is wrong for any to criticize them. "Who will say unto him, What doest thou?" (Job 9:12; see also Rom. 9:20–21). It would be well to remember, in the first place, that God is an all-wise God; secondly, that there will always be mystery surrounding His designs; and thirdly, that it is daring impudence to arraign the Almighty before the bar of human reason.

A Never-Failing Will

God has eternally determined everything that comes to pass. While our plans cannot ensure anything, His plan always finds fulfilment. It never founders. It never fails. By omnipotence, He puts His will into effect. That is what we are given to understand in the Scriptures. In Isaiah 46:9–11, for example, God says, "There is none else; I am God, and there is none like me…saying, My counsel shall stand, and I will do all my pleasure…yea, I have spoken it, I will also bring it to pass; I have purposed it, I will also do it." Clearly, God's counsel precedes His work: "My counsel shall stand" is followed by "I will do all my pleasure."

That counsel, or purpose, is said to be eternal. The apostle Paul wrote of "the eternal purpose" (Eph. 3:11). It follows that "known unto God are all his works from the beginning of the world" (Acts 15:18). God has decreed from eternity what will take place in time; hence, He has always had detailed knowledge concerning future events. And since God is eternally the same, it is necessary to speak of His will as absolute, depending upon nothing (Ps. 135:6) and unchangeable, so fixed as to allow no deviation; Hebrews 6:17 speaks of "the immutability of his counsel." Included within God's decree are all the acts of men. As we read in Proverbs 16:9, "A man's heart deviseth his way: but the LORD directeth his steps." Even the seasons of people's lives have been arranged (Ps. 31:15), as have the bounds of their dwelling places (Acts 17:26). So-called "chance happenings" are not what they seem to be: They are predetermined events that for wise but inscrutable reasons are essential to the fulfilling of God's plan. As Solomon once said, "The lot is cast into the lap; but the whole disposing thereof is of the LORD" (Prov. 16:33). Perhaps we can now begin to understand why James tells us not to say, "To day or to morrow we will go into such a city..." and so on, but rather to say, "If the Lord will, we shall live, and do this, or that" (James 4:13, 15).

A Glorious and Perfect Will

God's sovereignty is indeed absolute, but it is always exercised in harmony with His glorious attributes and perfections. By this word *absolute* we mean that all things decreed will certainly happen. On its own, this truth could make God seem severe, and His will extremely hard and oppressive. The Bible relieves us of such fears by assuring us that sovereignty has certain qualities. We will outline some of these below.

Infinite Wisdom

Wisdom affects both God's will and His actions. As we read in the prophecy of Isaiah, the Lord is "wonderful in counsel, and excellent in working" (28:29). God's wisdom, which far surpasses human wisdom, is displayed in the formation of all the divine and eternal plans: "The LORD is a God of judgment [always doing what is right]: blessed are all they that wait for him" (30:18).

Perfect Justice

People may sometimes question God's justice, but God decrees everything according to the strict laws of equity. Hence the words of Job 34:10: "Far be it from God, that he should do wickedness; and from the Almighty, that he should commit iniquity." Dealing with the doctrine of predestination, Paul asked, "Is there unrighteousness with God?" He immediately answered his own rhetorical question: "God forbid" (Rom. 9:14). In God's sovereignty, it is true that He wills to *permit* evil, but this does not mean that He forces men to sin (Acts 14:16; Rom. 1:21–32). Futhermore, His purpose to allow sin does not make sinners any less responsible or accountable (Matt. 26:24; Acts 2:23–24).

Why doesn't God, as Almighty, prevent sin from ever taking place? The answer can only be that God intends to turn sin to His people's good and to His own glory. We read in Genesis 50:20, "But as for you, ye thought evil against me; but God meant it unto good"; and Psalm 76:10 speaks to the same issue, saying, "Surely the wrath of man shall praise thee: the remainder of wrath shalt thou restrain." When, at the last, all is revealed, we will be able to rejoice with all the saints in heaven, saying, "Great and marvellous are thy works, Lord God Almighty; just and true are thy ways, thou King of saints" (Rev. 15:3).

Great Goodness

Goodness is that perfection of the divine nature that issues forth in kindness and generosity. As the psalmist told the Lord, "Thou art good, and doest good" (Ps. 119:68). Goodness may be common (shown to all men), or special (shown to only some, the elect [Ps. 145:9; Lam. 3:25]), but it is still goodness, and it affected God in the making of His eternal plans. We conclude that divine sovereignty is best understood within the context of the divine perfections.

The Means of Displaying God's Sovereignty

This great attribute of God is displayed for all to see. The Bible speaks of God's sovereignty being displayed in three ways: creation, providence, and redemption.

Creation

In accordance with His sovereign will, God created the heavens and the earth. The Bible opens with the words "In the beginning God." This is a foundational statement, declaring that no one suggested to God that He should create, and certainly no one put pressure upon Him, obliging Him to act in this way. "In the beginning *God* created the heaven and the earth" (Gen. 1:1, italics added). By His own word, He spoke this universe into being: "He spake, and it was done; he commanded, and it stood fast" (Ps. 33:9). The praises of heaven acknowledge this. Creation is attributed to a sovereign God. "Thou art worthy, O Lord, to receive glory and honour and power: for thou hast created all things, and for thy pleasure they are and were created" (Rev. 4:11).

Providence

Sovereignty is also evidenced in the works of providence. God orders everything that takes place in this world. He "worketh all things after the counsel of his own will" (Eph. 1:11). What does that mean but that God has determined to control and guide the whole universe? Earthly rulers may boast of their power, but it is God's prerogative to bring to pass whatever He pleases. "Who is he that saith, and it cometh to pass, when the Lord commanded it not?" (Lam. 3:37). Why, our Savior told His disciples, not even a "sparrow" can "fall on the ground without your Father" (Matt. 10:29).

Redemption

Finally, sovereignty is demonstrated in the accomplishment of redemption. Paul, the inspired apostle, wrote in one of his letters that "all things are of God, who hath reconciled us to himself by Jesus Christ" (2 Cor. 5:18). God Himself declares, "I will have mercy on whom I will have mercy, and I will have compassion on whom I will have compassion" (Rom. 9:15). We will expand on this vital point below.

The Display of God's Sovereignty in Salvation

God displays His sovereign working in every aspect of the salvation of believers. There is nothing for us to boast of. From God's decree in eternity past, through the calling and justifying of sinners and their assurance, perseverance, and entrance into glory, from beginning to end, all the glory must go to Him. One could write at length on the way God works at every stage. Here, however, we will highlight only a few points.

The Eternal Decree

The scheme of our salvation was devised from all eternity. Conceived in the heart of God, it lay hidden in the depths of the divine counsels. The gospel of Jesus Christ now reveals this mysterious plan in its full glory. As Paul wrote, "We speak the wisdom of God in a mystery, even the hidden wisdom, which God ordained before the world unto our glory" (1 Cor. 2:7). Foreseeing the ruin of the whole of humanity, God freely and graciously chose a multitude from the rest of mankind and predestined them to a complete and everlasting salvation. Scripture says, "God hath from the beginning chosen you to salvation" (2 Thess. 2:13; see also Eph. 1:4; 1 Thess. 5:9). This was God's heart's desire; it pleased Him to do it. God formed this whole design; man had nothing to do with it. In impressive sovereignty, God decided to save sinners. That salvation was entirely gracious and "according to the good pleasure of his will" (Eph. 1:5, 9).

Special Revelation
Special revelation is the redemptive self-disclosure of God, which is now cast into the permanent form of Holy Scripture. In particular, it is the gospel of our Lord Jesus Christ. God has sovereignly chosen to communicate with people in this way. He was not obliged to do so; He graciously willed to make Himself known. God has broken the silence and "spoken unto us" (Heb. 1:2). Now, the gospel is called "the gospel of God" because God is responsible not only for sending it into the world, but also for sending it to particular people. The psalmist was aware of this, saying, "He sent his word, and healed them" (Ps. 107:20). Paul pointed out to the Jews in Pisidian Antioch, "to you is the word of this salvation sent" (Acts 13:26).

Distinguishing grace is wonderfully in evidence here. In God's providence, the gospel is denied to some and granted to others. There is a singular example of this in the book of Acts. Paul and his associates were "forbidden of the Holy Ghost to preach the word in Asia." They therefore turned north to the region of Mysia, thinking that they might enter Bithynia, a province on the southern shore of the Black Sea, but "the Spirit suffered them not." Then, in a vision, Paul saw a Macedonian, who said, "Come over into Macedonia, and help us." The next day, when Paul told the others about this, they all came to the same conclusion: "the Lord had called us for to preach the gospel unto them [i.e., the Macedonians]" (Acts 16:6–10).

The gospel is not sent just to a country, or even to a community; it is sent to certain individuals. Our Lord referred to the fact that although in Elijah's day, "many widows were in Israel," that prophet was sent "unto Sarepta, a city of Sidon" to minister to one particular "woman that was a widow." Similarly, when Elisha was prophet, there were "many lepers in Israel," but Elisha brought Jehovah's favor to only one: "Naaman the Syrian" (Luke 4:25–27). These examples serve to remind us of God's sovereign right to bestow His benefits on whomever He pleases.

Effectual Calling

God's sovereign call is through the gospel, but by the power of the Spirit is also "according to his own purpose and grace" (2 Tim. 1:9; see also Rom. 8:28, 30). While some sinners are left in their unbelief, others—the elect—are powerfully affected by the Holy Spirit. They are convinced of their sin and misery, enlightened in the knowledge of Christ, and then persuaded to trust in the Lord for salvation. "Thy people," says the psalmist, "shall be willing in the day of thy power" (Ps. 110:3). While the gospel call may prove ineffective, this mighty call by the Spirit of God is always successful. In apostolic teaching the "called" are one and the same as the "saved" (1 Cor. 1:18, 24). The chosen are "called…out of darkness into his marvellous light" (1 Peter 2:9).

Effectual calling is not deserved; neither is it brought about by man. It is a sovereign act of God. Writing of his own experience, Paul said, "It pleased God, who separated me from my mother's womb, and called me by his grace, to reveal his Son in me" (Gal. 1:15–16). See where it begins: "It pleased God." It did not please the sinner; the sinner was in open revolt, resisting every divine overture. "It pleased God." There are actually two wills in conflict here: the will of the sinner who says, "I will not come," and the will of Almighty God who says, "But you will come." And the will of God prevails. The sinner comes.

I remember reading of a simple man who expressed a desire to be a communicant member of a Scottish kirk, or church. Interviewed by the kirk elders, he was asked, "How did you come to an experience of salvation?" The poor young man answered, "Well, I think it was like this: in my salvation, I played a part and God also played a part." As you can imagine, the elders were none too happy with that reply, and I think they were more or less ready to terminate the interview. However, the young man continued by saying, "Sirs, my part was to do everything I could to refuse Christ. God's part was to do everything necessary to make me a Christian!" And, of course, that is exactly how it is. Irresistible grace does not mean that the sinner never resists. It means that although he does resist, God overcomes his wicked resistance and works so powerfully that, in the end, a bitter enemy is made a loyal subject of our Lord and Savior Jesus Christ.

Sanctification

Sanctification is ascribed to God. Polluted sinners cannot sanctify themselves. Hence, we read: "the very God of peace sanctify you wholly" (1 Thess. 5:23). Included in the eternal purpose was the intention of making the elect "holy" and "without blame" (Eph. 1:4). God fulfils His purpose in initial sanctification (or regeneration) and then in progressive sanctification. As Scripture says, "It is God which worketh in you both to will and to do of his good pleasure" (Phil. 2:13). The good works of believers are not only foreordained (Eph. 2:10), they are effected by the sovereign grace of God. "LORD," said the prophet Isaiah, "thou also hast wrought all our works in us" (Isa. 26:12). So, if we have reached any degree of holiness, it is the result of divine activity. Each one of us is constrained to say with the apostle Paul, "By the grace of God I am what I am" (1 Cor. 15:10).

Our Entrance into Glory
The apostle Paul rejoiced over his future prospects. "And the Lord," he said, "shall deliver me from every evil work, and will preserve me unto his heavenly kingdom" (2 Tim. 4:18). As for the apostle Peter, he was absolutely persuaded that an "entrance" would be "ministered" to us "into the everlasting kingdom of our Lord and Saviour Jesus Christ" (2 Peter 1:11). When at last we reach that glorious realm, we will ascribe our presence there to the sovereign power of a sovereign God. As we approach the eternal throne, we will rejoice to know that we are in heaven, not by free will but by free grace, and free grace alone. Along with all glorified men and women, we will sing: "Salvation to our God which sitteth upon the throne, and unto the Lamb" (Rev. 7:10).

The Right Response
Inevitably, this doctrine will have a profound effect upon us as Christian believers. In fact, it should change every aspect of our lives. The discovery of these truths from the Word of God inevitably affects the approach we have to God in public worship, that special time of the gathering of the church to reverence His

name. Also, it changes the whole tenor and attitude of our daily living, so that we are always conscious of the one we represent. Let us examine our hearts to see whether we are responding in the right way to these awesome truths of the Scriptures.

Worshiping with Reverence

When we have a right view of the divine sovereignty, we will approach God with appropriate reverence. Psalm 5:7 teaches the need for holy awe. David said, "But as for me, I will come into thy house in the multitude of thy mercy: and in thy fear will I worship toward thy holy temple." Similarly, Psalm 89:7 tells us that "God is greatly to be feared in the assembly of the saints, and to be had in reverence of all them that are about him." So if a church believes in a sovereign God, its worship will be markedly different from the worship commonly found in contemporary Christian churches. There will be godly humility, mixed with an awe of the holy. People will rejoice with trembling. Moreover, a church with this faith will make sure that every element of its worship is prescribed in the Scriptures, for it will want God's approval, not His disapproval.

Submission to His Authority

The knowledge of a sovereign God will move us to submit to His authority and observe His commandments. It was said of Job first that he "feared God" and then that he "eschewed evil" (Job 1:1). Job's profound sense of God's sovereignty made him dread sin and choose the way of righteousness. David confessed, "I have set the LORD always before me" (Ps. 16:8). He constantly bore in mind that God observed him and witnessed his every action. This, more than anything else, influenced how he lived.

Reaching the Elect

In this doctrine lies the great motivation for sharing the gospel. God has a people to gather—a people to save for eternity. Remember that when Paul was at Corinth, he was much discouraged by the general response to his preaching. The Lord then appeared to him and said, "I am with thee.... I have much people in this city" (Acts 18:10). Christ reminded him of God's sovereignty, which had been exercised in election. In that city were many precious souls who had to hear the truth and believe in the Lord Jesus Christ. They had to experience the salvation of God. It was written in the eternal decree. This was the main reason why it was necessary for Paul to stay: Through his preaching, the elect would be saved.

Sadly, modern churches appear ignorant of this doctrine. Many of them have become so discouraged that they have given up on mission. Others have reached the conclusion that biblical methods are no longer appropriate. These are the fruits of Arminianism, the theology that arose at the opening of the seventeenth century and opposed, among other things, the doctrine of election and predestination. However, believing in the sovereignty of God, we continue to preach the Lord Jesus Christ as the only savior of sinners. We firmly believe that God will own such preaching and that it will be as in the first century, when "as many as were ordained to eternal life believed" (Acts 13:48).

Fellowship and Love for the Saints

We know that God has predestined His people to eternal life, and that they will therefore certainly enjoy that life. Consequently, we feel a very special bond with all that are the objects of His saving grace. We reason like this: If God has loved them with an everlasting love, it ill becomes any of us to fall out with them or to be estranged from them. True, we may sometimes have to disagree; we may even reach the point where we have to separate. But we should certainly avoid unnecessary division. How can we justify the needless breaking of fellowship with God's people, who are chosen by the Father, redeemed by the Son, and called by the Holy Spirit?

Contentment with Providence

This doctrine of sovereignty ministers great comfort and strength to all who believe it. Since God is sovereign, and since all things are done according to His purpose, it surely becomes us to submit to His providential dealings and His arrangement of our particular circumstances. A sovereign God should not be questioned, nor should His will be criticized in any way. Some two hundred years after Scottish Presbyterian Samuel Rutherford penned his letters and sermons, Anne Ross Cousin wove Rutherford's words into a beautiful piece of poetry. One of her verses reads as follows:

> *With mercy and with judgment*
> *My web of time he wove,*
> *And aye the dews of sorrow*
> *Were lustred with his love.*
> *I'll bless the hand that guided,*
> *I'll bless the heart that plann'd,*
> *When throned where glory dwelleth*
> *In Immanuel's land.*[2]

Rutherford knew that the experiences of his life, and even his troubles and griefs, came through the fingers of a gracious God.

---

2. Samuel Rutherford, *Letters of Samuel Rutherford* (Edinburgh: Banner of Truth, 1984), 743.

His bitter disappointments were therefore God's wise appointments. Grace taught him to recognize this, and so to be content. The Bible speaks of "godliness with contentment" (1 Tim. 6:6).

Christians should not speak in terms of "misfortune" or "accident," and certainly they should not speak of "fate." Scripture reports that when Aaron lost his two sons, he simply "held his peace" (Lev. 10:3). Similarly, when Eli was told of the death of his sons and the removal of the priesthood from his family, he is reported to have said, "It is the LORD: let him do what seemeth him good" (1 Sam. 3:18). Job suffered severe affliction and bereavement, yet from his lips came those remarkable words: "The LORD gave, and the LORD hath taken away; blessed be the name of the LORD" (Job 1:21). Now, this is where Calvinism becomes such a support. However fearful the storm, Calvinists always see the Pilot at the helm. We know that we are not at the mercy of the elements. Instead, we are in the care of our God. Should He guide us into trouble, it is only to fulfill a loving purpose and to bestow a special blessing. How precious are the words of Jeremiah 29:11: "I know the thoughts that I think toward you, saith the LORD, thoughts of peace, and not of evil, to give you an expected end"—or, as the margin has it, "an end and expectation." This sovereign God orders all our experiences for our spiritual good, that we might be conformed to the image of His dear Son and so be made fit for the glory which soon we will enter and enjoy.

> *Goodness and mercy all my life*
> *Shall surely follow me:*
> *And in God's house for evermore*
> *My dwelling-place shall be.*[3]

---

3. *Scottish Psalter*, 1650, Psalm 23, verse 5.

Hope in the Promises

God's sovereignty has a great effect upon our hope. In times of doubt and uncertainty, we fall back upon His eternal purposes of love. The believer reasons in his heart like this: "Has God not called me through the gospel? Did He not justify me and give me the sweet sense of sins forgiven?" If these things are true, the golden chain of Romans 8 will not be broken, and I may recite these words to express my confident expectation: "Whom he called, them he also justified: and whom he justified, them he also glorified" (v. 30). The God of grace and glory will bring His people to heaven, there to behold the resplendent glory of His Son and to enjoy the blessed fellowship of His triumphant church.

Calvin used to begin Sabbath worship with the words of Psalm 124: "Our help is in the name of the LORD, who made heaven and earth" (v. 8). Our help is in the same sovereign Lord. These words lead us to another psalm in which we read a wonderful promise: "The LORD shall preserve thee from all evil: he shall preserve thy soul. The LORD shall preserve thy going out and thy coming in from this time forth, and even for evermore" (Ps. 121:7–8). The doctrine of the sovereignty of God is the leading doctrine of the Reformed faith. In life, in death, and through all eternity, we will lift up our voices and say, "Alleluia: for the Lord God omnipotent reigneth" (Rev. 19:6).

May God grant this experience in our hearts, thereby encouraging us in our way until, in life's last hour, we prove its strength to support us in the river of death and bring us safely to the land of promise. Amen!

CHAPTER 3

A Right View of Worship

Whoso offereth praise glorifieth me.
—Psalm 50:23

"What is worship?" This is a question of great importance today, when so much confusion is evident among professing Christians. The Westminster Shorter Catechism declares in its first sentence that "man's chief end is to glorify God,"[1] and God Himself says to us in the psalms, "Whoso offereth praise glorifieth me" (Ps. 50:23). How vital it is, then, for us to grasp this issue of worship and rightly fulfil the purpose for which God made us, preserved us, and redeemed us. There is surely no greater work on earth or in heaven than this.

Worship is the reverence and homage that we render to the Supreme Being, through means such as praise, prayer, the reading of Scripture, and the preaching of the Word of God. "Reformed worship" is worship that is strictly according to God's written Word, which is "the only rule to direct us how we may glorify and enjoy him."[2] It includes everything authorized by Scripture, and it excludes everything not authorized by Scripture. Calvin stated the biblical and Reformed view of

---

1. The Shorter Catechism, in *Westminster Confession of Faith*, 287.

2. The Shorter Catechism, 287.

worship when he wrote this: "We are not to seek from men the doctrine of the true worship of God, for the Lord has faithfully and fully instructed us how he is to be worshiped."[3]

The Object of Worship

God's perfection entitles Him to the honor of our worship. In Isaiah 6:1–3, we read of Isaiah's vision of the Lord enthroned on high in His temple. The seraphim were present with their faces covered, and they were admiring that glory which separates and distinguishes Him from all others. "Holy, holy, holy, is the LORD of hosts: the whole earth is full of his glory." Men and women entertain similar thoughts, for they too are aware that no one can be brought into comparison with Jehovah. "There is none like unto thee, O LORD; thou art great, and thy name is great in might. Who would not fear thee, O King of nations?" (Jer. 10:6–7). Such infinite glory deserves some external expression of our inward veneration. Soul and body must unite in this service, for if the soul is not involved, it is mental atheism, and if the body is not involved, it is practical atheism. The Lord Jesus declared, "Thou shalt worship the Lord thy God, and him only shalt thou serve" (Matt. 4:10). The apostle Paul delivered this exhortation to believers: "Glorify God in your body, and in your spirit, which are God's" (1 Cor. 6:20).

In worship, our intention should be to give, not to get. The Psalms teach that to "give unto the LORD the glory due unto his name" is one and the same as to "worship the LORD in the beauty of holiness" (Ps. 29:2). This is taken up in another psalm, but with these additional words: "bring an offering,

---

3. Calvin, *Institutes,* 4.10.8.

and come into his courts" (96:8). This will be the spiritual offering of prayer and praise (1 Peter 2:5), presented not because He has need of it, but because it is an important part of our "reasonable service" (Rom. 12:1). However, the assistance of the Holy Spirit is essential to a right performance of this duty. The Spirit reveals the mysterious, unsullied splendor of our God. Again the psalmist comes to our aid here with this image: "For with thee is the fountain of life: in thy light shall we see light" (Ps. 36:9). It is only by the Spirit's enlightenment and illumination that we are able to see, through faith, the God of glory. Such spiritual sight evokes the response in our hearts that is necessary to true worship. Furthermore, as worshipers, we need the Holy Spirit to aid us in the preparation and presentation of our worship. Remember Paul's words in his epistle to the Ephesians: "And be not drunk with wine, wherein is excess; but be filled with the Spirit; speaking to yourselves in psalms and hymns and spiritual songs, singing and making melody in your heart to the Lord" (5:18–19).

We can expect great spiritual profit in the worship of God. After all, worship is really drawing near to Him who is our highest good. It is even more than that. It is enjoying His presence, increasing our knowledge of Him, and rejoicing in sweet communion with Him. "It is good for me to draw near to God: I have put my trust in the Lord GOD, that I may declare all thy works" (Ps. 73:28). When Moses saw the burning bush as he traveled through the back of the desert, he turned aside to look more closely, and on that holy ground, God declared Himself to Moses. This is an instructive passage, teaching us that in worship we discover more of our blessed God.

The Way of Worship

Reformed theology declares that only God has the right to determine the true and proper mode of worship. He has clearly prescribed this in His Word. The law of worship is that only what God has prescribed in Scripture may be introduced into His worship, or, to put it in another form, what Scripture does not prescribe, it forbids.

Today there is a great deal of confused thinking about worship. Some people think that we can adopt any mode of worship, provided that God has not expressly forbidden it in His Word. In practice, this allows for many human corruptions and abuses. Where in Scripture are we forbidden to use particular vestments? To bow toward the east? To make the sign of the cross? To read from the Apocrypha? To kneel at the Lord's Table? It is clear that this principle is entirely unsatisfactory. It allows for practically anything in divine worship. However, the scriptural law of worship is not that we can do whatever is not forbidden, but rather that we can do only what is clearly prescribed. When this regulative principle is faithfully applied both outwardly and inwardly, the result will be the recovery of pure and spiritual worship. The Word of God clearly teaches this Reformed view of worship.

Biblical Teaching on Worship: The Old Testament

The moral law of God, summarized in the Ten Commandments, authoritatively states the rule that should govern worship. In the first commandment, God declares Himself to be the only one who should be worshiped. In the second, He requires that believers observe only those institutions that He has divinely appointed: "Thou shalt not make unto thee any graven image" (Ex. 20:4). As sovereign Lord, it is

God's prerogative to order His own worship, and He makes it clear that there is no place for the inventions of men ("*Thou* shalt not make *unto thee*"). In the Hebrew, that word we read translated as *make* means "constitute" or "appoint." So in the second commandment, God is prohibiting human beings from devising or observing anything in worship which He has not instituted. It is as if God is saying, "I am the Lord God, and I alone order My worship. People are not at liberty to introduce their devices into worship without My command."

In accord with this law, God prescribed in great detail all the various aspects of Israel's worship. In the tabernacle, and later in the temple, God insisted on appointing everything. You may recall the words delivered to Moses and recorded in Exodus 25:40: "And look that thou make them after their pattern, which was shewed thee in the mount." Israel's lawgiver received inspired and specific directions about the tabernacle and its service. These directions addressed such matters as the coverings, the boards, the sockets, the veil, the ark, and so on. Human ingenuity had nothing to do with it; divine regulation covered the whole of tabernacle worship. It was precisely the same with the temple. In 1 Chronicles 28:11–12 we read that "David gave to Solomon his son the pattern"—that is, the pattern for the temple and its worship. David received these instructions by divine revelation, for it was "the pattern of all that he had by the spirit." Once again, God exercised His right to arrange His worship, allowing no room for human innovations.

Scripture contains detailed written prescription of the mode of His people's worship. This is obvious from the book of Leviticus, which is all about various rites and ceremonies in worship. What impresses us at once is its amazing detail. Many of the regulations concern the duties of the priests, ritual sacrifice, the distinction between clean and unclean animals, ceremonies of purifications, and the observance of sacred days and seasons. God appears to be constantly saying, "This must be done, and that shall be done!" Leviticus 6:9, for example, begins this way: "Command Aaron and his sons, saying, This is the law of the burnt offering." Then verse 14 says, "This is the law of the meat offering," and verse 25 says, "This is the law of the sin offering." God made laws to govern the entire system of divine worship.

God's Command to Man

Deuteronomy 4:2 states, "Ye shall not add unto the word which I command you, neither shall ye diminish ought from it, that ye may keep the commandments of the LORD your God which I command you." This verse and verses 13 to 19 refer to worship. What the Lord is saying through Moses is this: "In worship there must be strict adherence to the inspired and written Word; there are to be no additions and no subtractions." Calvin commented on Deuteronomy 12:32 as follows: "By forbidding the addition, or diminishing of anything, he plainly condemns as illegitimate whatever men invent of their own imagination."[4] It was in connection with worship that this solemn question was asked: "Who hath required this at your hand?" (Isa. 1:12). The immediate reference is to the people's irreverent trampling (with their cattle) of the sacred enclosures surrounding the temple. This practice had not been authorized. It was therefore regarded as a terrible profanation or desecration. God deeply resented

---

4. John Calvin, "Harmony of the Last Four Books of Moses," in *Calvin's Commentaries* (Grand Rapids: Baker, 1993), 2:453.

that such a thing was being done, chiefly because He had not sanctioned it in His Word.

What if we applied this to the evangelical scene at large? "Who hath required this at your hand?" We enter a typical modern church only to be confronted with an orchestra and, more than likely, with a set of drums. "Who hath required this at your hand?" The service begins, and before long there is some kind of dramatic presentation; perhaps a parable or miracle is acted out. "Who hath required this at your hand?" A woman then rises to read a poem that she has written. People are moved—but, "Who hath required this at your hand?" The sermon turns out to be a series of images on the overhead projector. "Who hath required this at your hand?" And so we could proceed. The question, however, remains. "Who hath required this at your hand?"

God deeply resents it when in worship, people act independently of Him, without any reference to His revealed will. In Jeremiah 7:31 He censures their conduct: "And they have built the high places of Tophet, which is in the valley of the son of Hinnom, to burn their sons and their daughters in the fire; which I commanded them not, neither came it into my heart." It was not simply that they had engaged in an offensive building enterprise. It was not even that they had performed numerous cruel rites. It was, rather, that they were doing in their worship what God "commanded them not." God indicts them for the same kind of thing in Jeremiah 19:5 and 32:35. Understandably, therefore, the godly took great care to keep to prescribed arrangements. Hence we read in 2 Chronicles 8:12–13 that Solomon "offered burnt offerings…even after a certain rate every day, offering according to the commandment of Moses." Something very similar is written of David in 2 Chronicles, namely, that "he set the Levites in the house of the LORD with cymbals, with psalteries, and with harps...for so was the commandment of the LORD by his prophets" (29:25).

Believers today would do well to keep to God's prescribed arrangements. Of course, if we do follow them, we will be in the minority. Most of our evangelical contemporaries are prepared to tolerate all kinds of entertaining innovations in public worship. Our solemn duty, however, is to obey God. We must, first of all, stand fast ourselves. Then we must call others—professing Christians and professing churches— back to God, the Scriptures, and God's holy commandments. The modern church is causing God great offense. It is ignoring Him and behaving as if there were no rule for worship.

Worshiping Our Own Way

We should not be surprised to find that God has repeatedly and consistently judged those who have worshiped Him according to their own devices. Take the case of Cain. Immediately after the Fall, God graciously revealed the gospel, and then illustrated it by means of a sacrificial offering (Gen. 3:15, 21). The offering that Abel subsequently brought was such as God had required, "the firstlings of his flock and of the fat thereof" (4:4). However, Cain's offering was not the specified blood sacrifice, but "the fruit of the ground" (4:3). The Bible says that the Lord accepted Abel's worship and rejected Cain's. In fact, the way of Cain ultimately led to banishment from God.

Leviticus 10:1–3 tells of Aaron's two sons, Nadab and Abihum, priests who offered "strange fire" before the Lord. God had enjoined that coals should be taken from the brazen altar, the altar of sacrifice, to provide fire to burn incense on the golden altar (Lev. 16:12; see also Rev. 8:5). This was an important and deeply significant command, because it linked sacrifice with intercession. For some reason, Nadab and Abihu obtained coals from elsewhere. They offered "strange fire" when burning the incense. This was offering what "[God] commanded them not." God was so angry with them that "there went out fire from the LORD, and devoured them, and they died before the LORD." How careful we should be about what we offer in worship! We must always choose revelation over reason. If we are inattentive to the divine commandments, God will take no pleasure in us, and may deal with us severely.

Biblical Teaching on Worship: The New Testament

When we come to the New Testament, the first thing we should observe is that just as Moses was faithful in ordering the worship of the Jewish church, Christ has been faithful in ordering the worship of the Christian church. Our Lord, we read, was "faithful to him that appointed him, as also Moses was faithful in all his house [that is, in every particular of his house]" (Heb. 3:2). If words mean anything, this means that just as Moses prescribed every detail of ancient ceremonial, typical worship, so Christ has given precise instructions regarding every part of new covenant spiritual worship. Of course, the Mosaic institutions were "shadows" or "figures" of the good things to come, and, of necessity, they had to be set aside and to be superseded by new elements of worship more appropriate to the new order. Christ therefore delivered new laws and ordinances for the gospel church, and Christian believers are told to "hear ye him" (Matt. 17:5). Although there has been a change, God still reserves the right to arrange His worship, and Christians should scrupulously adhere to the directions of His Word.

"In Spirit and in Truth"

During His ministry, the Lord Jesus Christ plainly taught that worship must be "in spirit and in truth" (John 4:24). Now, what exactly did He mean by that? He meant that worship in the Christian era must be in keeping with the nature of God ("in spirit"), and it must also be regulated by His revelation ("in truth"). Worship "in truth," the British Baptist Dr. John Gill observed in the 1700s, is worship "according to the word of truth and agreeable to his will."[5] This stipulation, in particular, excludes all human innovations in evangelical worship. Christ made clear that the mode and form of worship had changed. An altogether new way of worship had been introduced, but that new way of worship is determined by God's Word. God's Word is still the rule from which there must not be any deviation. If we turn away from the Word of God, perhaps believing that there is now a new freedom, we have it on Christ's authority that our worship will become "vain" or "useless." This kind of worship will not render homage to God at all, but rather to men! In the gospel of Matthew, we read that Christ asked the Jews, "Why do ye also transgress the commandment of God by your tradition?" (15:3). The verb *transgress* literally means "go beyond"; it suggests an overstepping of the boundary. This is exactly what is happening today. Dissatisfied with biblical worship, people wish to indulge their own "go-ahead" views. They claim to be breaking new ground, and they boast of their contemporary worship. Yet we fear it is all to no real spiritual profit. The Lord Jesus Christ says it is "in vain."

---

5. John Gill, *Gill's Commentary* (Grand Rapids: Baker, 1980), 5:633.

The application of this principle is hard, very hard, and both minister and people need much grace from God if they are to act upon it. We find it difficult to accept that some things that we have been doing for years lack the necessary scriptural authorization; we also find it difficult to change our worship in ways that make us quite different from the other evangelical churches around us. However, the point of gathering on the Sabbath is not to please ourselves. We gather on that day to please Almighty God. We must endeavor to present before His throne what He has required of us; otherwise, we shall miserably fail in our worship. In His Great Commission, our Lord emphasized this and taught that He would appoint every part of His church's worship. "All power," He said, "is given unto me in heaven and in earth. Go ye therefore, and teach all nations, baptizing them in the name of the Father, and of the Son, and of the Holy Ghost: teaching them to observe all things whatsoever I have commanded you" (Matt. 28:18–20). His ministers, therefore, have the responsibility to teach professing believers to obey only what the Lord commands. Christ gave some commandments personally, and others through His apostles (John 14:25–26; 16:12–13; 2 Cor. 13:3). Either way, we are bound to practice that worship and keep those ordinances that He has appointed in His Word. Calvin said of this passage, "He sends away the apostles with this reservation, that they shall not bring forward their own inventions, but shall purely and faithfully deliver from hand to hand [as we say] what he has entrusted to them."[6]

---

6. Calvin, "Commentary on a Harmony of the Evangelists" in *Calvin's Commentaries*, 17:390.

In perfect accord with what Christ said, the apostles made clear that the Word alone should determine what is to be done in church worship. For example, Paul gave direct instructions about the ordinance of the Lord's Supper. "For I have received of the Lord," he wrote to the Corinthians, "that which also I delivered unto you"; and he then proceeded to tell the Corinthians, in detail, how the sacrament should be administered and received (1 Cor. 11:23–30). Later in the same epistle, he insisted that their public worship services be properly conducted, and laid out the specifics: Only their appointed teachers were to take part, and just two or three "prophets" (or inspired teachers) were to speak, "one by one" (14:29–31).

Paul maintained that God's Word should determine the form of church worship. He totally rejected the idea that the church itself could prescribe anything relating to its worship. Authority, he insisted, does not come from the church; it comes *to* the church, in God's inspired and inerrant Word. "What? came the word of God out from you? or came it unto you only?" (1 Cor. 14:36). Scripture is the authority brought to bear on the church. "If any man think himself to be a prophet, or spiritual, let him acknowledge that the things that I write unto you are the commandments of the Lord" (1 Cor. 14:37). And that is the way it should be. Worship must not be ordered by the ideas of a man, nor by the will of a congregation. Worship must be ordered by the Scriptures, and only by the Scriptures.

"Will Worship"

We are solemnly warned about the danger of being led astray from God's Word. Modern, innovative worship may appear spiritual and attractive to some, but we should remember that Scripture says that in the final analysis, some things which have "a shew of wisdom" constitute "will worship" (Col. 2:23). What exactly is "will worship"? It is a form of worship that proceeds from our own ingenuity. Paul criticizes it as the practice of false doctrine. As William Young put it, "The will of God, not the will of man, is the rule of the worship of the New Testament Church."[7] In some modern churches, worship seems at first sight to be grand: There are choirs, dancers, orchestras, and much more besides. Yet there is no authority for any of these things in the New Testament. What is it, then? It is "will worship"!

Our Lord Jesus Christ instituted worship for the whole Christian era. He did this immediately during His own public ministry and mediately through the subsequent teaching of His apostles. As His people, we are obliged to follow His instructions and reform our worship in the light of His revealed will. Worship should include the singing of psalms; readings from the Old and New Testaments; prayers of thanksgiving, supplication, and intercession; preaching of the Word of God; blessing in the name of the Lord (the benediction); and the observance of the two sacraments, baptism and the Lord's Supper. See then that you are circumspect in these things. Make God's Word the sole rule in all matters of public worship. God has said, "Them that honour me I will honour" (1 Sam. 2:30). May God be worthily praised in all the churches!

> All nations whom thou mad'st shall come
> And worship rev'rently
> Before thy face; and they, O Lord,
> Thy name shall glorify.

---

7. William Young, *The Biblical Doctrine of Worship* (Pittsburgh: Reformed Presbyterian Church of North America, 1974), 314.

Because thou art exceeding great,
And works by thee are done
Which are to be admir'd; and thou
Art God thyself alone.

Teach me thy way, and in thy truth,
O Lord, then walk will I;
Unite my heart, that I thy name
May fear continually.[8]

---

8. *Scottish Psalter*, 1650, Psalm 86, verses 9–11.

CHAPTER 4

The Government of the Church

The keys of the kingdom.
—Matthew 16:19

In England in 1643, both Houses of Parliament and the Westminster Assembly of Divines gave assent to the document known as the Solemn League and Covenant. One witness described the atmosphere as the draft document was read to the Assembly: "Our smoking desire for uniformity did break forth into a vehement flame, and it was so heartily embraced, and with such a torrent of affectionate expressions, as none but eye and ear witness can conceive."[1] The covenant bound its subscribers to endeavor to reform religion "in doctrine, worship, discipline and government, according to the word of God, and the example of the best reformed churches."[2] It also bound them to seek "the extirpation [complete removal] of Popery, Prelacy, (that is, church-government by Archbishops, Bishops, their Chancellors, and Commissaries, Deans, Deans and Chapters, Archdeacons, and all other ecclesiastical

---

1. Thomas McCrie, *The Story of the Scottish Church* (Glasgow: Free Presbyterian Publications, 1988), 195–96.

2. Solemn League and Covenant, in *Westminster Confession of Faith*, (Inverness: F. P. Publications, 1981) 358.

Officers depending on that hierarchy), superstition, heresy, schism, profaneness, and whatsoever shall be found contrary to sound doctrine and the power of godliness."[3]

We can learn much from the zeal of those Christians to conform themselves to the pattern of the Scriptures in every respect. They would not lie content with partial reformation, but sought for every aspect of the life of the church to be brought into submission to the will of God. We need to be reminded that Christ is the only lawgiver in our churches; we must be clear on the nature of the authority which He has delegated to church officers, and what type of men He would have to serve Him in these offices. This is in contrast to the practice of many churches today. The government of the church is often seen as a secondary issue, and there appears to be little desire to strive after biblical church government.

Basic Principles of Church Government
The Lord Jesus Christ Is Sole Head of the Church
A number of biblical passages expressly declare Christ's headship. A prophecy in Isaiah refers to Him as a "prince," and explains this to mean that "the government shall be upon his shoulder" (Isa. 9:6). Another prophecy, this time in Micah, describes Him as "ruler in Israel," who will "feed [rule] in the strength of the LORD, in the majesty of the name of the LORD his God" (Mic. 5:2, 4).

In the New Testament, such prophecies find their fulfilment. Ephesians 1:22–23 states that after God had "put all things under his feet," He "gave him to be the head over all things to the church, which is his body, the fulness of him that

---

3. Solemn League and Covenant, 359.

filleth all in all." So, by virtue of Christ's office as mediator, He
has a general, universal sovereignty that He exercises for the
sake and benefit of His church. However, as the apostle Paul
made clear, Christ also has special lordship or dominion over
His church: "He is the head of the body, the church" (Col.
1:18). His various titles confirm this. He is called "king," as
in Psalm 2:6: "Yet have I set my king upon my holy hill of
Zion." He is called "shepherd," which also denotes authority;
the prophet says of Him that "He shall feed his flock like a
shepherd" (Isa. 40:11). In the New Testament, He calls himself "master" (John 13:13), and His disciples regularly call him
"Lord," even "Lord of all" (Acts 10:36). Hebrews 3:6 describes
Him as "son over [God's] own house; whose house are we":
that is, God's Son, exercising His authority over the church of
the living God. So His titles show that He is indeed the head
of the church.

Further confirmation may be found in His official acts
or works. We read that during the forty days between His
resurrection and ascension, "through the Holy Ghost" Jesus
delivered "commandments unto the apostles." These commandments concerned "the kingdom of God"—that is, they
were instructions about the organization of the Christian
church (Acts 1:2–3). They related to the institutions and
ordinances of the church. We know that Christ ordained the
preaching of the Word and those ordinances which are called
"sacraments," but He no doubt also spoke to the apostles
about the government of His church. Although the apostles
were leaders in their own right, their authority was not original; they could only minister in Christ's name. He alone was
head of what He rightly called "*my* church" (Matt. 16:18).

Christ Has Established a Government in the Church

Scripture frequently uses the word *key* as a symbol of government (Isa. 22:22; see also 9:6). While absolute and total power of government belongs to Christ (Rev. 3:7), He evidently conferred some power upon His apostles, who exercised it according to His revealed will. In the days of His flesh, He said to Peter, "I will give unto thee the keys of the kingdom of heaven" (Matt. 16:19; see also 2 Cor. 10:8; 13:10). Since a key locks or unlocks a house, this was a symbolic way of stating that Peter and the other apostles could grant or deny the right of access to the church, according to people's response to the gospel.

The apostolic office was, of course, extraordinary, and by reason of its nature, it was temporary (Acts 1:21–22; 1 Cor. 4:9—margin). But Christ instituted other "government offices" that are ordinary and permanent. "When he ascended up on high, he…gave gifts…. He gave some, apostles; and some, prophets; and some, evangelists; and some, pastors and teachers" (Eph. 4:8, 11). We learn in 1 Corinthians 12:28 that "God hath set some in the church, first apostles, secondarily prophets, thirdly teachers, after that miracles, then gifts of healings, helps, governments, diversities of tongues." Christ's visible kingdom requires government, and the Lord's will concerning this has been fully made known in His Word (1 Tim. 3:14–15).

Church Authority Belongs Only to Some

The titles associated with government are given to certain individuals in the church. These are *elders*, *bishops* (or *overseers*), *rulers*, *governors*, and *shepherds*. Other terms refer to the rest of the church community, such as *kingdom*, *city*, *family*, and *flock*. It is clear that the divine arrangement calls for some believers to take leadership among the Lord's people.

This is clear from the names used, and also from the spiritual gifts bestowed upon them. We read in Ephesians 4:11–12, in a passage similar to 1 Corinthians 12:28, that Christ "gave some, apostles; and some, prophets; and some, evangelists; and some, pastors and teachers; for the perfecting of the saints, for the work of the ministry, for the edifying of the body of Christ" (v. 12).

Furthermore, there evidently are spiritual duties that only some are intended to perform. The duty of preaching the Word, for example, is entrusted to such as are called: "How shall they preach, except they be sent?" (Rom. 10:15). Administration of the sacraments is another duty that belongs to men ordained by the Lord: "Go ye therefore, and teach all nations, baptizing them…teaching them to observe all things whatsoever I have commanded you" (Matt. 28:19–20; see also Acts 16:15, 33; 20:11). We might also mention here the ordination or setting apart of men to the Christian ministry. Paul wrote to Timothy, "Neglect not the gift that is in thee, which was given thee by prophecy, with the laying on of the hands of the presbytery" (1 Tim. 4:14). The entire church did not lay on hands. A distinct group of men within the church, the "presbyters," performed this act of blessing. Our English word *presbyter* comes from the Greek *presbuteroi*, which is often translated "elders." The presbyters, or elders, had the authority under Christ to set others apart to this sacred office.

These examples make it clear that in apostolic times, not every church member exercised power or authority. It was something exercised by regularly appointed officials within the church. An unhappy development in nonconformity has been the widespread adoption of a democratic spirit. In some churches it is now assumed that one member has as much right as another to lead and to rule, to preach the Word, or to preside at the Lord's Table. This is totally unwarranted. Indeed, it is plainly contrary to the Holy Scriptures.

The Divine Right (Jus Divinum) *of Church Government*

Our forefathers used the term *jus divinum* to convey that the church's government is by divine right or law. In other words, God's written word plainly and fully sets it forth. During the Reformation, of course, there were men such as Bishop Stillingfleet of Worcester, who argued that the New Testament does not prescribe any particular church order. They maintained that bishops or civil magistrates should decide what form of government was best. Inevitably, the preferred government was by archbishops, bishops, and priests. Puritans and Covenanters would not accept this, since they were convinced of the need for further reformation in doctrine, worship, and government and, in the case of the Covenanters, they were prepared to swear to adhere to and defend the true religion. They did not believe that Christ had left His church to be ordered according to human whims. Turning to the New Testament, they found no sign of prelacy, but they did find strong evidence of government by presbyters.

Church Power Must Be Spiritual

To avoid misunderstanding, let us state the obvious: Within the church, power is spiritual. When we speak of power in government, some might understand that to mean dictatorship—the very opposite of what the New Testament teaches and requires. Rule within the church must correspond to the spiritual nature of Christ's kingdom. Jesus said, "My kingdom is not of this world: if my kingdom were of this world, then would my

servants fight" (John 18:36). The nature of the kingdom determines the nature of its leadership. But what exactly is meant by
"spiritual" rule?

Church government must be prescribed by the Spirit-
breathed Scriptures (1 Tim. 3:1–7). It must be appointed by
the Holy Spirit of God (Acts 20:28) and exercised by men who
have the mind of Christ, and who evidence the fruit of the
Spirit: "Brethren, if a man be overtaken in a fault, ye which
are spiritual, restore such an one in the spirit of meekness"
(Gal. 6:1). Church government must always be spiritual. The
presbyters or elders should always bear in mind that they are
dealing with souls—souls God loves. Therefore, they must
show great care for them, healing their wounds, binding them
up, and strengthening them. The ultimate objective will be
spiritual, too. Elders should function only to please God and
to benefit His people. Their purpose is to produce holiness
and to remove sin: "For this is the will of God, even your sanctification" (1 Thess. 4:3).

Scriptural Government Is for All Time

We are not to think that the pattern laid down in the Scriptures was meant only for the early church. It is clear from our
Lord's own words that it was meant to be permanent, lasting
to the end of time. In His Great Commission, our Lord said,
"Go ye therefore, and teach all nations, baptizing them in the
name of the Father, and of the Son, and of the Holy Ghost:
teaching them to observe all things whatsoever I have commanded you: and, lo, I am with you always, *even unto the end
of the world*" (Matt. 28:19–20, italics added).

This is also clear from apostolic teaching. The New Testament epistles teach that biblical offices are to continue in the

church until their end is attained—that is, until all believers are made fully perfect (Eph. 4:11–13). The arrangements of the ministry and government of the church (1 Tim. 3:1–15; 5:17–22) are to be preserved "without spot, unrebukeable, until the appearing of our Lord Jesus Christ" (1 Tim. 6:14).

Government Is for the Well-Being of the Church
It can be shown from the Scriptures that a church can exist without proper biblical government. In Acts 14, for example, Paul and Barnabas are said to have "ordained them elders in every church" (v. 23). This means that before any such appointments were made, believers already had gathered and formed churches. Churches without officers are not ideal, however, and what is lacking should be supplied as soon as possible (Titus 1:5). It is therefore important to make a distinction between a church's *being* and its *well-being*.

The Office of Elder
The New Testament uses two titles for those in government. One is *presbyter*, which we colloquially also call *elder*. The other title is *bishop*.

The term *elder* indicates the kind of men most suited to this office. They are not to be immature, inexperienced, or lacking in wisdom. They are not to be new converts, unproven in doctrine and service. Instead, they should evidence solid Christian character and should have earned the respect of the believing community.

We get the English word *bishop* from two Greek words: *epi*, which means "over," and *skopeo*, which means "to see" or "watch." A bishop is an overseer. This name describes the nature of the work associated with the office: responsible superintendence. Bishops, according to the apostolic writings, are the guardians and keepers of the church.

Scripture uses the two terms interchangeably to denote the same office. In Acts 20, for example, Paul called the Ephesian "elders" to Miletus, and then addressed them as "overseers" (vv. 17, 28). In his letter to Titus, he called the officials "elders," but then referred to one of them as "a bishop." Reminding Titus of his duty to "ordain elders in every city…if any be blameless," Paul went on to say, "For a bishop must be blameless, as the steward of God" (1:5–7). Both terms also appear in 1 Peter 5. Here, Peter exhorted "the elders," urging them to exercise "the oversight" (that is, the function of bishops) (vv. 1–2).

There were many such officers in each of the early churches. We can see that from the inspired record in the book of Acts. Paul and Barnabas revisited the churches in Lystra, Iconium, and Antioch, and "ordained them elders in every church" (Acts 14:23; see also James 5:14). Later, Paul wrote to the church at Philippi, addressing the members (called "saints" or "consecrated ones") and also the officers, the "bishops and deacons" (Phil. 1:1). Such texts prove beyond doubt that each church or congregation had several governing officers.

The Duty of Elders: To Rule

It is the responsibility of a bishop or elder to rule. Among the Jews, the office of elder was always associated with government. If we go right back to the beginning of Israel's history, we will find that elders presided over the affairs of the entire nation. God spoke to Moses and said, "Go, and gather the elders of Israel together" (Ex. 3:16). These men, the elders of Israel, were the recognized leaders of the Jewish people (see, for instance, 1 Sam. 4:3). In Mosaic law there is evidence of a certain development. A law dealing with a murderer required "the elders of his city" to "deliver him into the hand of the avenger of blood, that he may die" (Deut. 19:12). These elders had a more restricted responsibility; they were guardians of the law in one particular city.

Although the Old Testament does not go into detail about the government of the synagogues, in the New Testament we discover that a council of elders led each one. Synagogues, we believe, were of divine institution. Leviticus 23:3 refers to Sabbath "convocations" or "assemblies" (see also Ps. 74:8; Luke 4:16). The gospel of Mark calls Jairus "one of the rulers of the synagogue" (Mark 5:22; see also Acts 13:15). This is important because the synagogue was destined to be the cradle for the pattern of the Christian church (see James 2:2—margin). As there were elders or rulers in the synagogue, so officers were appointed in each of the apostolic churches. Other New Testament references to governments speak of "them which…are over you in the Lord," and "them that have the rule over you" (1 Thess. 5:12; Heb. 13:17).

First Timothy 5:17 confirms this: "Let the elders that rule well be counted worthy of double honour, especially they who labour in the word and doctrine." What do elders do? They rule, and, according to this verse, they should rule well. Other names used for elders in the New Testament reinforce this. Earlier, mention was made of Titus 1:7: "For a bishop must be blameless, as the steward of God." A steward is someone appointed by the owner of a house to be its director or manager. This involves the idea of rule. Peter encouraged elders to take "oversight" and to "feed the flock"; the implication is that they are called to be under-shepherds to Christ, "the chief Shepherd" (1 Peter 5:1–4). What does a shepherd do?

A shepherd takes responsibility for the sheep. He leads and guides them. In the Old Testament, the term *shepherd* denotes "a prince" or "ruler" (Isa. 44:28; Ezek. 37:24; Mic. 5:5 — margin) and "to feed" is one and the same as "to govern" or "rule" (1 Chron. 11:2; Mic. 7:14 — margin).

The qualifications of an elder likewise suggest the concept of rule. A bishop or elder must be "one that ruleth well his own house, having his children in subjection with all gravity," for, as that Scripture goes on to say, "if a man know not how to rule his own house, how shall he take care of the church of God?" (1 Tim. 3:4–5) Further confirmation may be found in the commands delivered to these men. They are told to be "overseers," or managers, of the church (Acts 20:28), but because their position and function might lead them to abuse their powers, they are told not to be heavy-handed: "Neither as being lords over God's heritage, but being examples to the flock" (1 Peter 5:3). What can this mean but that the nature of their office is to rule and that they are to rule worthily? The actions of the elders demonstrate the point quite conclusively. In the council at Jerusalem, they determine what should be done (Acts 15:4, 22); apparently, they are invested with authority. Subsequently, the same group of men takes the initiative to avert a real danger, and they even put forward a proposal to the apostle Paul (Acts 21:18–25).

Teaching Elders and Ruling Elders: An Important Distinction
We have established that all elders are appointed to rule. Some, but not all, exercise a public teaching ministry as well. That is the historical position, but can it be shown to be scriptural? Yes, I believe it can.

The New Testament teaches that there are officers who simply govern. In Romans, for example, Paul particularly mentioned "he that ruleth" and urged that this duty be performed "with diligence" (12:8). Now, this does not mean that only such officers ruled, but it does mean that they were wholly set apart for that important function. A supporting verse is 1 Corinthians 12:28, where Paul wrote, "God hath set some in the church…governments." This appears near the end of a list of extraordinary and ordinary officers, and as in Romans, it makes a distinction between "teachers" (the elders who taught in public) and "governments" (the elders whose role was to rule). The fact is, these tasks require different gifts. There is a gift of teaching, and there is also a gift of ruling. This much is clear from Ephesians 4:8–11, in which Paul alluded to Christ's ordinary and permanent gifts, and pointed out that Christ has given "pastors and teachers." It does not say "some pastors and some teachers," but rather "some, pastors and teachers." The wording in the Greek indicates that these two functions can be conjoined in the same persons. So, why did Paul refer to pastor-teachers? It was so readers would understand that some elders rule and also serve as official teachers. It is plain that all the offices mentioned in verse 11 are associated with verbal communication. There were apostles, prophets, and evangelists, all of whom were called to preach; and there were also, within the local churches, "pastors and teachers." This set of men possessed not one but two special abilities, and as a result, they pastored the flock, and they also preached the Word. This shows that the apostle recognized two different gifts, ruling and teaching, which may or may not be possessed by the same persons.

An important verse in this connection is 1 Timothy 5:17. There we read: "Let the elders that rule well be counted worthy of double honour, especially they who labour in the word and doctrine." This verse plainly teaches that some elders restricted themselves to government, while others, besides their governing work, were devoted to a public preaching ministry. In Hebrews 13:7 we have the words, "Remember them which have the rule over you." Which kind of elders did the writer have in mind? Evidently teaching elders, for the passage continues, "who have spoken unto you the word of God." Verse 17 mentions the elders again, but this time it simply says, "Obey them that have the rule over you." The words used earlier—"who have spoken unto you the word of God"—are now omitted. Why? It is surely because, in the second place, the apostle is not referring to teaching elders, but to ruling elders. Thus, in his final exhortations, he preserves the distinction within the eldership.

The Minister of the Word

The minister of the Word should be the presiding officer. If we could cite only 1 Timothy 5:17, that would be sufficient to support the point we are making: "Let the elders that rule well be counted worthy of double honour, *especially* they who labour in the word and doctrine" (italics added). The word *honor* means "respect," and special respect is to be given to those who devote themselves to the ministry of the Word. Why is this? It is because this officer is appointed to lead the church in the way of obedience to the Lord's revealed will. Of course, this teaching elder does not exercise authority for his own sake, nor does he make himself a lord over the consciences of others. He simply presents the Word and leads the church into humble and holy obedience to God.

As we have already seen, the government of the early church followed that of the Jewish synagogue. There were several elders in each synagogue, but one of them appears to have been recognized as "the ruler of the synagogue" (Luke 13:14). Crispus, for example, is described as "the chief ruler of the synagogue" and, on his conversion to Christianity, Sosthenes apparently succeeded him in that office (Acts 18:8, 17). Who was this "chief ruler"? He was sometimes called *scheliach tsibbor*, a Hebrew name answering to the word "angel" or "messenger" (see Rev. 2:1, 8, 12, 18; 3:1, 7, 14). According to the Jews, this person was none other than the minister of the synagogue. A famous rabbi of the twelfth century believed him to be the presbyter who "laboured in the word and doctrine."[4]

Certainly, in the New Testament, the public teacher is given higher status than other governors and rulers (1 Cor. 12:28). He is one whom the Lord has specially "sent" to "preach" (Rom. 10:15), and, as a result, he has greater authority (Titus 2:15). While the elders generally will "shepherd the flock," the teacher will always be recognized as the "pastor" (Eph. 4:11).

Responsibilities of Teaching Elders

Take general charge of the church. According to our Lord's teaching, the "scribe…instructed unto the kingdom of heaven" is very much like a "householder" (Matt. 13:52). In fact, he is the "faithful and wise servant" who the Lord has made "ruler over his household, to give them meat in due season" (Matt.

---

4. Samuel Miller, *Letters Concerning the Constitution and Order of the Christian Ministry* (New York: Hopkins and Seymour, 1807), 1:65.

24:45). We learn from the letters to the seven churches that the "angel" or "messenger" has the main responsibility for the church. If something goes sadly wrong, he is the one who will be held to account for it (Rev. 2:5, 14–15; 3:2, 17).

Faithfully teach the truth. As the "pastor-teacher" (Eph. 4:11), he must concentrate on the work of "teaching" (Rom. 12:7). Indeed, his special employment is to "labour in the word and doctrine" (1 Tim. 5:17). That is onerous work, and before criticizing any minister, perhaps one should reflect on the great difficulties of his calling. He has to preach week in and week out and often four or five times in a week. This means hard study and constant prayer, because for each sermon or lecture he needs new material and a fresh anointing of the Holy Spirit. Only so will he be able to meet the needs of his people, leading them in their spiritual pilgrimage, building them up in their holy faith, and comforting them in their souls.

Administer the sacraments. He must administer the sacraments in the right manner and to the proper persons. When the apostles—those extraordinary preachers—were commissioned, they were sent not only to teach men, but also to baptize them and bring them to "observe" whatever else Christ had appointed (Matt. 28:19–20). Hence, we find that they baptized people and administered the Lord's Supper. Paul, for example, baptized the Philippian jailer and his family, and at Troas he presided at the breaking of bread (Acts 16:33; 20:11).

Pray for the church. Like the apostles in Acts 6:4, he must give himself to prayer. In a sense the apostles were teaching elders, albeit extraordinary teaching elders. Both Peter and John, for example, used this title for themselves (1 Peter 5:1; 2 John 1:1; 3 John 1:1). Paul can also be considered a teaching elder. Read of how he prayed for the believers at Ephesus: "I bow my knees unto the Father of our Lord Jesus Christ…that he would grant you, according to the riches of his glory, to be strengthened with might by his Spirit in the inner man" (Eph. 3:14–16; see also Phil. 1:4, 9; Col. 1:3, 9; 1 Thess. 3:10; 2 Thess. 1:11). Ministers should have a ministry of intercession. They should pray for their churches.

Assist those in trouble or sorrow. The role of being a help to the needy was perfectly fulfilled by the Great Teacher, who was given "the tongue of the learned" so that He could "speak a word in season to him that is weary" (Isa. 50:4). Taking Him as the great exemplar, the apostle Paul could remind the Thessalonians that he and his fellow workers had been "gentle" among them, "even as a nurse cherisheth her children" (1 Thess. 2:7). That spirit must be in the teaching elder as he performs his ministry by "rightly dividing the word of truth" (2 Tim. 2:15). The thought here seems to be that the minister must act like the head of the family at mealtimes, supplying each person with the word that he or she may need.

Defend the church against evil. Teaching elders must watch for any sign of approaching danger (Ezek. 3:17; Isa. 62:6; 2 Tim. 4:5). They must "preach the word; be instant in season, out of season; reprove, rebuke, exhort with all long suffering and doctrine" (2 Tim. 4:2).

Set a godly example. The teaching elder must live out his doctrine, thereby confirming it to his congregation. Timothy was told, "Be thou an example of the believers, in word, in conversation, in charity, in spirit, in faith, in purity" (1 Tim. 4:12). It is true that actions speak louder than words. One of the reasons the Lord has set the teaching elder in the church is that he might be "a pattern of good works...that he that is of the contrary part may be ashamed, having no evil thing to say of you" (Titus 2:7–8). Yes, a minister will have his enemies, but the manner of his life should be such as will silence them, and so prevent them from casting any reproach upon our Christian faith. To the faithful within the church he must be a true "man of God" (2 Tim. 3:17), his very presence being a blessing; then his ministry will be to great spiritual profit. Scripture says that Barnabas was "a good man, and full of the Holy Ghost and of faith," and we read that as a result, "much people was added unto the Lord" (Acts 11:24).

The Responsibilities of Ruling Elders
Lead church members to observe the whole revealed will of Christ. It was perhaps the church at Jerusalem that received this apostolic injunction: "Obey them that have the rule over you, and submit yourselves" (Heb. 13:17). Of course, the assumption is that the ruling elders will lead the church in a clear scriptural direction. The church is not obliged to follow them if they do otherwise. In such a case the church must "obey God rather than men" (Acts 5:29). However, if they lead in the way of God's Word, it is incumbent on the church to obey.

At times, there may be a difference of opinion between the elders and the members. It is not necessarily so that the elders are recommending anything contrary to the Scriptures. It is just that whether a given matter is fairly unimportant or extremely problematic, there can be different views about the best way to proceed. What happens if some members do not share the views of the elders? According to Hebrews 13:17, the members should "submit" or yield to the elders. They should recognize that the Lord has appointed the elders as the rulers of the church.

Be responsible for admissions and exclusions in the church. It was to the Ephesian elders that the apostle Paul said, "Take heed therefore unto yourselves, and to all the flock, over the which the Holy Ghost hath made you overseers." He warned that after his "departing," "grievous wolves" would "enter in," and also that from among their "own selves," some would actively "draw away disciples after them." In the light of this, Paul told the elders to "watch" (Acts 20:28–31). Why tell the elders to do that? The reason is to make it clear that it was their responsibility to receive members into the church, and exclude others. The Lord has entrusted elders with "the keys."

Set apart men for office. In 1 Timothy 4:14, mention is made of "the laying on of the hands of the presbytery" (or eldership). This took place when someone was designated to a special work. It was therefore used in the appointment of both deacons and elders (Acts 6:5–6; 1 Tim. 5:22). The laying on of the hands of the elders is an act of public and formal recognition. It marks the bestowal of the necessary gifts and authority. It shows a man to be set apart, or designated, to office.

Watch over the behavior of members. Remember the words of 1 Thessalonians 5:12–13: "And we beseech you, brethren, to know them which labour among you, and are over you in the Lord, and admonish you; and to esteem them very highly in

love for their work's sake. And be at peace among yourselves."
A duty of elders is to take oversight of the Lord's people and
promote a greater degree of knowledge and holiness (1 Tim.
3:5; 1 Peter 5:1–3). If evil breaks out in immorality, heresy,
or strife, elders must exercise corrective discipline in order
to remove such offenses. This may mean private or public
rebuke. It may mean suspension from special ordinances. It
may even mean the highest censure of all: the solemn exclusion from the fellowship of Christ's church. These actions
are certainly warranted by Holy Scripture, and they are also
absolutely necessary to a church's spiritual well-being.

Judge matters relating to doctrine or practice. In Acts 15, when
there was a controversy over whether circumcision was indis-
pensable to salvation, Paul, Barnabas, and other brethren,
went up to Jerusalem unto "the apostles and elders" (v. 2), and
"the apostles and the elders came together for to consider of
this matter" (v. 6). As a result of their deliberations, they were
able to reach a decision, which was relayed by letter to other
churches (vv. 22–33). The principle is clear: When a matter
is raised that seems crucial to the purity and peace of the
church, it falls to the elders to discern what is true and right.
They should then give direction to the church.

Care for the souls of the people. Scripture clearly teaches that
elders should visit those in need, ministering to them physi-
cally and spiritually. "Is any sick among you? let him call for
the elders of the church; and let them pray over him" (James
5:14). Maybe, after reading the Scriptures, an elder should
minister with a word of encouragement or exhortation
(1 Timothy 3:2 notes that a bishop must be "apt to teach"), or

it may be necessary for him to lead an individual to repentance and a closer walk with God (Gal. 6:1–2). Elders must act spiritually, ever remembering that the Lord has entrusted them with precious, redeemed, and immortal souls.

Endeavor to remove strife and division. In his first letter to the Thessalonians, Paul urges believers to respect their elders. He then adds the clause "and be at peace among yourselves" (5:12–13). This is not an independent exhortation, with no connection to what precedes it. The apostle's point is that elders will always be concerned to preserve the unity of the church, and if the members regard them as they should, they will do everything in their power to prevent estrangement and disruption. Our Savior commanded this (Mark 9:50), no doubt because "where envying and strife is, there is confusion and every evil work" (James 3:16).

The Character Required of Elders
Elders must be true men of God. They must be in union and communion with Christ, which is why Paul wrote of exercising oversight "in the Lord" (1 Thess. 5:12). He meant that elders must be in fellowship with the Lord, knowing His love in their hearts and His blessing on their lives. They must also evidence grace in godly and holy lives. Our Lord taught that only a "good man" is able, "out of the good treasure of the heart," to bring forth "good things" (Matt. 12:35). Among the qualifications for elders or bishops given in 1 Timothy 3, one requires such men to be "blameless" (v. 2). In other words, no one should be able to point a finger at them and accuse them of serious inconsistency in living the Christian life. That is not to say, of course, that they must be perfect. It is to say, however,

that they must not have any obvious substantial defects in character or conduct. Their authority to lead the members in the way of obedience to God obviously depends to a very large extent on their own consistent behavior. "Remember them which have the rule over you," we are told in Hebrews 13:7, where the verb *to rule* literally means "to lead" or "guide." The implicit message is that elders should show others the right path by taking that path themselves. They must lead the church by both teaching and example.

Lastly, elders must possess the necessary spiritual gifts. They must have a sure grasp of the truth, understanding the doctrine taught in inerrant Scripture. As the apostle Paul phrased it in one of his letters, elders must be known for "holding fast the faithful word" (Titus 1:9). Furthermore, they must have the ability to impart their knowledge to others. Elders should be able to instruct the ignorant and to re-educate the misguided. Paul's reference in 1 Timothy 3:2 to elders' aptitude for teaching refers not to public preaching, but to private conversations, as is clear from the only other use of the expression in the New Testament: "And the servant of the Lord must not strive; but be gentle unto all men, apt to teach, patient, in meekness instructing those that oppose themselves; if God peradventure will give them repentance to the acknowledging of the truth" (2 Tim. 2:24–25).

They should also possess and exercise the gift of government. The ability to take charge, or care, of the church is named as one of the spiritual gifts (1 Cor. 12:28; Rom. 12:6, 8). Elders must be responsible persons who hold strong biblical convictions, and who are prepared to carry those convictions through. Yet they must also be able to persuade (not cajole) church members to follow them in doctrine and

practice. Their role is to shepherd the flock, and to success-
fully fulfill that role, they must have a good relationship with
their people and be known for their kindness and wisdom.
They must also excel in that fairly rare gift of tact that will
enable them to know just when and how to deal with various matters. What need there is for elders to offer Solomon's
prayer: "Give therefore thy servant an understanding heart
to judge thy people" (1 Kings 3:9)! Blessed and happy is a
church that has such elders. It will surely enjoy God's presence and favor.

Should we not respect our elders, praying for them and
giving them our support? Ministers need prayer in order
that they may powerfully preach the truth. Ruling elders
need prayer to enable them to apply the truth to every area of
church life. Do nothing to discourage them in their arduous
and demanding work. Rather, do everything to encourage them, by your love, fellowship, and obedience. One of
God's greatest promises is, "I will give you pastors according to mine heart, which shall feed you with knowledge and
understanding" (Jer. 3:15). May the Lord fulfill that word
in our day, that our churches may recover their purity and
strength. Then will Christ receive rich revenues of honor
and praise.

> *When Sion by the mighty Lord*
> *Built up again shall be,*
> *In glory then and majesty*
> *To men appear shall he.*
>
> *The prayer of the destitute*
> *He surely will regard;*
> *Their prayer will he not despise,*
> *By him it shall be heard.*

For generations yet to come
This shall be on record:
So shall the people that shall be
Created praise the Lord.[5]

---

5. *Scottish Psalter,* 1650, Psalm 102, vv. 16–18.

CHAPTER 5

Reformed Church Discipline

Take heed therefore unto yourselves, and to all the flock, over the which the Holy Ghost hath made you overseers.
—Acts 20:28

Discipline is a word that requires definition. Derived from the Latin *disciplina*, it means "teaching." One definition of the term states that "discipline includes all those processes by which a church, as entrusted with the care of souls, educates its members for heaven."[1] Time and custom, however, have narrowed its sense so that it is generally understood to mean the proper treatment of offenses.

Warham Walker used an extended metaphor to make clear the full meaning of discipline:

A body of soldiers may be said to be well-disciplined, not when the court martial is constantly busy in repressing acts of insubordination among them, but when they are so generally observant of the order of their commander, and of all the military regulations under which they are placed, that there are few such acts to be suppressed. In speaking of the discipline of an army, we of course

---

1. Hezekiah Hervey, *The Church: Its Polity and Ordinances* (Rochester, N.Y.: Backus, 1982), 87.

embrace in our meaning the correction of military offences. But this is not the whole of our meaning. We include in it, also, that process of military instruction and training, by which soldiers are formed, and fitted for active and efficient service.[2]

A right understanding of church discipline, therefore, will include teaching the truth and dealing with offenses. It is usual to speak of two forms of discipline: preventive and corrective.

Preventive Discipline

Preventive discipline is very positive. It aims at securing obedience and vital godliness. There are a number of ways to achieve this type of discipline.

Public and Private Instruction

The minister will preach God's Word, making people familiar with the doctrines and duties of the Christian faith. He will challenge them to live worthy of that name by which they are called. He will comfort those who are finding things difficult, and he will warn those who are tempted to turn aside. Such ministry is intended for "the edifying [or building up] of the body of Christ" (Eph. 4:12). Along with his ruling elders, the minister will communicate instruction in private conversation. The word translated "apt to teach" in 1 Timothy is used in 2 Timothy 2:24–25 to speak of counseling those with various problems: "The servant of the Lord must…be… apt to teach…instructing those that oppose themselves." So,

---

2. Warham Walker, *Harmony in the Church: Church Discipline* (Rochester, N.Y.: Backus, 1981), 22–23.

they will remind the members of their responsibilities to love, serve, and worship the Lord.

Proper Administration of the Sacraments

Through the sacraments, the Lord's people are richly blessed, so that they cleave to the Lord and continue with their pilgrimage. Our Lord said to the apostles (and the teachers who followed them) that they were to be busy "teaching them [i.e., the disciples] to observe all things whatsoever I have commanded you" (Matt. 28:20). As they observed the various sacraments, they were spiritually strengthened.

Cultivation of the Spirit of Brotherly Love

It is important to encourage members of a congregation to care for one another. Christ taught His disciples to have "love one to another," and, as a result, there is a great emphasis in the epistles on "brotherly love" or "kindness" (John 13:35; Rom. 12:10; 2 Peter 1:7). This love will be expressed in comforting or strengthening others (1 Thess. 4:18; 5:11), and it may even be expressed in disapproval or warning: "Warn them that are unruly" (1 Thess. 5:14). It is all part of the work of avoiding potential problems. Such mutual helpfulness may keep some soul from wandering or falling, and it is therefore a vital part of biblical discipline.

Appointment to Church Work

Romans 12 contains the rich image of the church functioning like a human body with its various members. Now, a body will be healthy only if its members—the greater as well as the lesser—discharge their particular functions and perform their respective offices. We have a variety of gifts, and by

God's help, we are to use and improve them faithfully for the edification of the whole church.

If the elders are wise, they will be always on the watch and ready to offer opportunities for the development of various abilities. Members will find fulfilment in their service for the Lord, and that may well eliminate feelings of discontent that could break out in murmuring. "The Devil loves to fish in troubled waters," wrote the Puritan Jeremiah Burroughs. "He says, 'There is good fishing for me,' when he sees men and women go up and down discontented, and he can get them alone, then he comes with his temptations."[3]

Church responsibilities should not be given only to those who evidence certain gifts. There are services for all in Christian fellowship. When everyone feels he has a part to play, criticism and dissension are less likely to break out in the church.

Examples of Devotion and Loyalty

We should remember how the apostle Paul stressed to Timothy that he should be "an example of the believers, in word, in conversation, in charity, in spirit, in faith, in purity" (1 Tim. 4:12). A strong example of godliness will often prevent others from lapsing into some kind of grievous fault. Consistent holy behavior is a means of blessing to the Lord's people, for their establishment and growth in grace. If church officers are distinguished by their spiritual focus and holiness of life, that will have a truly beneficial effect upon the membership. There is something strangely contagious about these things.

---

3. Jeremiah Burroughs, *The Rare Jewel of Christian Contentment* (Edinburgh: Banner of Truth, 1979), 126.

If elders conduct themselves in a becoming manner during services and meetings, members will tend to follow suit. This will be the case not only in public but also in private, in the way we order our families and arrange our devotional times. Godly example is a tremendously important way to prevent sin and error from coming into the church.

Why Problems Come

The malignity of Satan, the pressures of the world, and the weakness of our natures make it inevitable that there will be problems in the church (2 Cor. 2:11; 1 John 2:16; Rev. 3:2). As the Westminster Confession states, "The purest churches under heaven are subject both to mixture and error."[4] In God's sovereign, loving, and wise purposes, He permits offenses to occur. The Lord Jesus said, "It must needs be that offences come" (Matt. 18:7). What are the divine intentions in allowing them to take place?

First, offenses try and prove the grace in the Lord's people. When Christ intimated to His disciples that there was about to be a terrible betrayal, they each began to examine themselves, and to ask, "Lord, is it I?" (Matt. 26:22).

Offenses also make it possible to identify those who are really faithful and stable. When trouble arises, mature Christians come to the fore. Paul taught that heresies or factions are necessary for this very reason, "that they which are approved may be made manifest among you" (1 Cor. 11:19). A corollary, of course, is that offenses provide an opportunity to distinguish hypocrites from genuine believers. "They went out from us," writes the apostle John, "but they were not of us...but

---

4. *Westminster Confession of Faith*, XXV, 5.

they went out, that they might be made manifest that they were not all of us" (1 John 2:19).

In some situations, offenses establish the church in the great doctrines of the faith. The problems at Antioch and elsewhere ultimately brought "consolation" to Christians who were also "confirmed" as to the truth (Acts 15:30–32).

Finally, offenses bring experience of Christ's gracious presence. When they occur, the Lord is near, with His "fan," to "throughly purge his floor" (Matt. 3:12). The Lord's hand is never closer to us than when He is pruning His vine to make it even more fruitful in holiness and righteousness.

Corrective Discipline

Corrective discipline is, in essence, the judicial process against those who transgress Christ's laws. Its purpose is to eliminate the offense or offenses. Before examining this, we should establish three important principles.

A Mark of a True Church

The first principle is that discipline is one of the "notes" or "marks" of a biblical church. In the Scots Confession of 1560, we find this clearly stated: "The notes...of the true Kirk of God we believe, confess, and avow to be, first, the true preaching of the Word of God, into the which God has revealed himself unto us.... Secondly, the right administration of the sacraments of Christ Jesus, which must be annexed to the word and promise of God, to seal and confirm the same in our hearts. Last, *ecclesiastical discipline uprightly ministered,* as God's Word prescribes, whereby vice is suppressed, and virtue nourished"[5] (italics added). There is no finer statement in the Reformed confessions, and it clearly reflects the view of the great Protestant Reformers. If one or more of these marks are missing from a church, there is a serious fault and a grave deficiency at the very least, and perhaps that congregation is not truly a Christian church.

God has empowered and ordered the church to exercise discipline; therefore, this cannot be considered an unimportant matter. In Matthew 18:17, we have the Lord's words: "Tell it unto the church." This is fundamental to a right understanding of discipline. There are certain practices which, when persisted in, must come before the local church court. This is something that the Lord has ordained. When Paul addressed the gross immorality in the Corinthian church, he instructed the church to deal with it "in the name of our Lord Jesus Christ" (1 Cor. 5:4). Among other things, this means "by the authority of our Lord Jesus Christ." The apostle stated the authority on which church discipline rests.

In his *Marrow of Theology*, William Ames emphasized that ecclesiastical discipline is "ordained and prescribed by Christ himself, Matt. 16:19; 18:15–17. It is therefore…of divine right and may not be taken away, diminished, or changed by men at their pleasure. Indeed, he sins against Christ, the Author and Ordainer, who does not all he can to establish and promote this discipline in the churches of God."[6]

Our Lord appointed discipline as an ordinance. His reason for doing so was that the church might thereby fulfil its mission

---

5. John Knox, *The Works of John Knox* (Edinburgh: Wodrow Society, 1841), 110.

6. William Ames, *The Marrow of Theology* (Grand Rapids: Baker, 1997), 199.

in this world. What a failure the church is when it lacks good order! Disunity inevitably appears, and Christian love can no longer be expressed. Furthermore, a lack of discipline within the church can be a stumbling block for others. It is nothing short of a tragedy when unbelievers are spiritually scandalized by what they see in the community of God's professing people. The church exists to reflect and declare the glory of God (2 Cor. 3:18; Eph. 3:21), and unchecked sin among the membership will militate against the fulfilment of that grand purpose and design. Indeed, without discipline, the church will never be prepared for the kingdom of heaven. Yet the faithful exercise of biblical discipline means that the church, as the Lamb's wife, is able to make herself "ready" (Rev. 19:7).

Authority in Each Local Church

The second principle is that the power of discipline has been delivered to each local church, as we learn in the gospels was true of the synagogue (John 9:22, 35; 16:2). Christ provided practical guidelines about what to do if someone commits an offense and then refuses to discuss it: "If he shall neglect to hear them, tell it unto the church" (Matt. 18:17). Here, "the church" must refer to a particular, local company of believers; this verse teaches that the problem should be laid before the local church's governing body. Other passages confirm that each church has the authority, under Christ, to exercise discipline. Paul directed the Corinthian church to take action immediately against an unrepentant offender (1 Cor. 5:4–5). He stated the principle that each church has the right and responsibility to deal with those who offend against the laws of God.

However, this authority is to be exercised through the church's lawfully called officers. Thomas Witherow, a nineteenth-century Presbyterian, wrote as follows:

> God bestows powers upon man, but these powers are always exercised through one or other particular organ to which a special function is assigned. He gives man, for example, the faculty of sight, but this faculty is attached to the eye, and can only be exercised through that exquisitely constructed organ.... So it is in the Christian society. Christ has endowed the Church with the power of rule, but that rule is exercised by the officers chosen by the Church, and acting in the Church under the authority and with the approval of Christ.[7]

This is undoubtedly the biblical position and one far removed from government along democratic lines.

As was mentioned in chapter 4 of this book, Christ said to Peter, "I will give unto thee the keys of the kingdom of heaven" (Matt. 16:19). Peter was the first authorized to use this authority. He used the key of *doctrine* when he opened the kingdom to both Jews and Gentiles (Acts 2:14–42; 10:1–48), and he used the key of *discipline* when he closed the kingdom to Ananias and Sapphira and to Simon the sorcerer (Acts 5:1–11; 8:18–21). This power to admit or exclude people from the church was not something that belonged only to Peter. Other apostles also had the power to "loose" (let into the kingdom) and to "bind" (shut out from the kingdom) (Matt. 18:18; see also John 20:23). Paul certainly exercised this power. We read that under his ministry, "the door of faith" was opened "unto

---

7. Thomas Witherow, *The Form of the Christian Temple* (Edinburgh: T. & T. Clark, 1889), 148.

the Gentiles" (Acts 14:27), while others such as Hymenaeus and Alexander were "delivered unto Satan, that they may learn not to blaspheme" (1 Tim. 1:20)—that is, removed from the church into the world which is Satan's domain.

The keys are now in the hands of teaching and ruling elders, whom Paul called "the steward[s] of God" (Titus 1:7). Therefore, they are responsible for all admissions and exclusions. As mentioned earlier, Paul addressed the Ephesian elders with these words: "Take heed...unto yourselves, and to all the flock, over the which the Holy Ghost hath made you overseers.... For I know this, that after my departing shall grievous wolves enter in among you.... Also of your own selves shall men arise, speaking perverse things" (Acts 20:28–30). These officers are rulers of the church household (1 Tim. 3:5; 5:17). It follows that they are the ones responsible for church discipline (1 Thess. 5:12–13). As appointed by our Lord Jesus Christ, members should "obey them" and "submit [themselves]" (Heb. 13:17). Why are two terms used here? A. B. Davidson commented: "Submit or yield suggests more than obey, implying that even should wills and opinions in regard to faith and practice not be altogether in harmony, the teachers are to be yielded to."[8]

Strict Adherence to God's Word

The third principle is that any disciplinary action must be in accordance with Scripture. The apostle Paul was very concerned that everything in the church should be done "decently and in order" (1 Cor. 14:40; see also 11:34; Col.

---

8. A. B. Davidson, *The Epistle to the Hebrews* (Edinburgh: T. & T. Clark, n.d.), 258.

2:5). John Owen once observed that order simply consists in observation of the rule. Scripture regulates procedures, and also lays out the manner in which those procedures should be followed. Discipline should be exercised with seriousness, fairness, and love.

Like preaching the Word and administering the sacraments, discipline is something done "in the name of our Lord Jesus Christ," a phrase indicative of His great authority (1 Cor. 5:4). The same verse refers also to "the power of our Lord Jesus Christ," which gives effect to any sentence delivered (see also Luke 5:17; 2 Cor. 12:9). These considerations alone should lead elders and members to act with the appropriate bearing and proper seriousness.

Strict impartiality is required, for "the wisdom that is from above is first pure, then peaceable, gentle, and easy to be intreated, full of mercy and good fruits, without partiality" (James 3:17). Even more to the point are the words in 1 Timothy 5:21, in which Paul, dealing with particular disciplinary matters, exhorted Timothy to be conscientious in the discharge of his duty and to take action "without preferring one before another, doing nothing by partiality." In other words, a minister or elder must avoid any improper bias. He must not extend preferential treatment because of a person's personality or family connections. He must not be influenced by a sense of obligation to that person. There must be neither prejudice nor favoritism. Church officers are to examine matters carefully and then judge rightly.

It will all be in vain without love. Sadly, ministers and ruling elders sometimes err on the side of severity, and display no mercy. That can never be justified. Love should always be the distinguishing feature of Christ's church. Discipline that is scriptural will be characterized by concern (2 Cor. 2:4), patience (2 Tim. 2:24), gentleness (2 Tim. 2:24), humility (Gal. 6:1), and mercy (Jude 1:22). The latter verse deserves special emphasis. "Of some have compassion, making a difference," Jude wrote. In other words, treat with special tenderness those who were overtaken in a fault and appear penitent, as opposed to others who are rebellious and hardened by their sin.

Why Corrective Discipline Is Necessary

Elders must understand that their church is not immune to offenses. If dealt with properly, these will be overruled to the church's spiritual good. Discipline must take place in order to prevent the dishonoring of the Lord Jesus Christ. The Bible is quite clear that "every one that nameth the name of Christ" should "depart from iniquity" (2 Tim. 2:19). If the church is the bride of Christ, then it becomes her to be beautiful and pure, even "a glorious church…holy and without blemish" (Eph. 5:27). Only so will she be "worthy of the Lord" (Col. 1:10).

The restoration of the offender is also a vital part of the discipline process. Subordinate to the glory of Christ and the purity of His church, the immediate end of discipline is the recovery of the erring believer. "Note that man," wrote Paul, "and have no company with him, that he may be ashamed" (2 Thess. 3:14). This recovery can come only through deep repentance, experience of forgiveness, recovery of the divine favor, enjoyment of spiritual privileges, and return to the service of God. The church must recognize the signs of penitence and respond appropriately. When the immoral man at Corinth was brought to grieve over his sin, Paul advised the church to "forgive him, and comfort him" (2 Cor. 2:7).

A church that does not exercise discipline will undoubtedly suffer. Unchecked evil can only spread (1 Cor. 5:6–7;
15:33), and sooner or later, it will bring about tragic division and confusion. "Carnal" conduct will evidence itself
in "envying, and strife, and divisions" (1 Cor. 3:3). We are
given to understand that the ultimate remedy for this kind
of extreme behavior is exclusion from all fellowship with the
church. Paul told the Galatians, "I would they were even cut
off which trouble you" (Gal. 5:12).

Even more serious is the fact that failure to discipline
will result in the forfeiture of divine favor. We see this in our
Lord's letters to the churches of Asia Minor. His message to
Pergamos, for example, expressed concern over that church's
toleration of bad doctrine and practice. He told them, "Repent;
or else I will come unto thee quickly, and will fight against
them with the sword of my mouth" (Rev. 2:16). However,
when there is godly discipline, the church is approved, and it
receives spiritual blessing. This makes its witness to the world
far more effective.

Private Discipline

Some offenses can be adequately corrected by instruction,
admonition, and exhortation. Indeed, that is the best way to
start dealing with such faults as spiritual weakness, declension,
sloth, neglect, and even disagreeableness (see, for example,
Rom. 15:1–2; Gal. 6:1–2; Phil. 4:1; 1 Thess. 4:11; Heb. 10:25).
Ordinary church members may give this teaching, for Paul
commended the Roman believers for being so "full of goodness" and "knowledge" that they were able to "admonish one
another" (Rom. 15:14). There seems to be precious little of this
in modern churches. How is it that certain people can spread

rumors about others and severely criticize their spiritual leaders without anyone saying a word to them? To listen in silence to such things is to be guilty of complicity with their sins. "Thou shalt in any wise rebuke thy neighbour, and not suffer sin upon him" (Lev. 19:17; see also Col. 3:16; Heb. 3:13; 10:25).

James Ussher once commented, "If any man seeing another (whose journey he knoweth) wander out of the way, if he should not admonish him, he might justly be accounted unnatural: much more we knowing all men think to journey toward heaven, if we see any go the wrong way...and do not admonish them, [we] are even guilty of their wandering."[9] There are times when a person should say to a fellow church member, "Look, I really don't think you should be talking like this. It is not edifying to you or to me. Let's change the subject." That kind of firm but gracious response would go a long way to restore an erring believer.

Scripture lays out how to deal with private offenses that one member commits against another: improper conduct, an unkind response, or perhaps simply bad feelings between two individuals. Christ's instructions are recorded in Matthew 18:15–17: "Moreover if thy brother shall trespass against thee, go and tell him his fault between thee and him alone: if he shall hear thee, thou hast gained thy brother." The aggrieved party should take the initiative. He should go and meet with the offender, not wait for the offender to come to him. In private, he should seek to convince him of his offense, and give him the opportunity to explain his behavior. Every effort should be made at this meeting to settle the matter in a friendly way.

---

9. James Ussher, *A Body of Divinity* (London: R. J., 1702), 384.

"But if he will not hear thee, then take with thee one or two more, that in the mouth of two or three witnesses every word may be established." If the first attempt at resolution proves unsuccessful, the offended party should not be so disheartened that he completely gives up on the erring brother. Rather, he should ask several responsible and respected believers to accompany him on another visit to this person. They might be able to reason more effectively and bring further pressure upon the offender to apologize and be reconciled. It is often the case that a man will listen to others who are not actually involved in the dispute. In any case, these friends will subsequently be able to establish the facts of the case (see Deut. 19:15).

"And if he shall neglect to hear them, tell it unto the church: but if he neglect to hear the church, let him be unto thee as an heathen man and a publican." Should this further attempt fail, then, and not until then, it should become a church matter. "Tell it unto the church" is not to be understood to mean "take it straight to a church meeting." The meaning is that it should now be brought into the *sphere* of the church. In other words, it should be brought to the attention of the governing body (the eldership, commonly called the session or consistory). The minister and ruling elders will do what they can, perhaps meeting with the parties separately, and also together. If the offender fails to respond to their exhortations and admonitions, they should direct the church to exclude this person from the membership.

Public Discipline

Church members who defiantly, obstinately, and persistently commit serious offenses are the proper subjects of formal church discipline. To fail to act on such is plain disobedience to the Word of God.

At Corinth, where government had effectively broken down, the Lord took things into His own hands. Paul told the Corinthians that as a result of their abuse of the Lord's Supper, many of them were "weak and sickly" and many others did "sleep"—that is, they had actually died (1 Cor. 11:30).

A public offense is not a personal matter between church members, but a scandalous breach of Christian truth or morality. Such an offense may be committed by a church officer, as Paul envisaged in 1 Timothy 5:19–20: "Against an elder receive not an accusation, but before two or three witnesses. Them that sin rebuke before all, that others also may fear." Or, an ordinary church member may commit it. This was the situation in the Corinthian church; an illicit liaison of a dreadful nature had taken place, and Paul advised the church to call a solemn assembly to administer the ultimate disciplinary action. "Therefore," he insisted, "put away from among yourselves that wicked person" (1 Cor. 5:13).

Offenses Requiring Immediate Action

In most cases it is right and proper to follow the usual course in disciplining a member. However, if the offense is of a highly aggravated character, the discipline may need to be immediate. This was evidently necessary with respect to the incestuous Corinthian. "For," Paul wrote, "I verily, as absent in body, but present in spirit, have judged already, as though I were present, concerning him that hath so done this deed." He then proceeded to tell them that "gathered together" in a church meeting, they should "deliver such an one unto Satan" (1 Cor. 5:3–5)—that is, unto the world dominated by him. Swift action is sometimes necessary to maintain the honor of the Lord Jesus Christ and the reputation of His church.

There are a number of serious offenses that the church should censure swiftly. One is the corruption of worship. "And what agreement hath the temple of God with idols?" (2 Cor. 6:16; see also Rev. 2:14–16). Another is the denial of sound doctrine, on which Paul acted decisively: "Holding faith, and a good conscience; which some having put away concerning faith have made shipwreck: of whom is Hymenaeus and Alexander; whom I have delivered unto Satan, that they may learn not to blaspheme" (1 Tim. 1:19–20; see also 1 Tim. 6:3–5). Paul advised the Thessalonian church to disassociate from members who abandoned godly living: "Now we command you, brethren, in the name of our Lord Jesus Christ, that ye withdraw yourselves from every brother that walketh disorderly, and not after the tradition which he received of us" (2 Thess. 3:6; see also 1 Cor. 5:11). He gave the same counsel about those within a local church who disrupt spiritual peace: "Now I beseech you, brethren, mark them which cause divisions and offences contrary to the doctrine which ye have learned; and avoid them" (Rom. 16:17; see also 2 Cor. 12:20). His advice regarding members who rejected the lawful authority of church leaders was that those leaders should "warn them that are unruly" (1 Thess. 5:14; see also Matt. 18:17).

Disciplinary Measures

There are three censures that may be inflicted on offenders: admonition, suspension, and exclusion.

Admonition

The ancient Jewish church recognized admonition as a step in the corrective process. The law of Moses, for example, stressed the need to reprove others for their faults (Lev. 19:17), and there are references to this in other parts of the Old Testament (Ps. 141:5; Prov. 27:5–6). However, such passages relate to believers in general and concern mutual care and correction, not formal church discipline. More relevant scriptures would be those that mention "him that reproveth [or rebuketh] in the gate" (Isa. 29:21; Amos 5:10)—the "gate" being the place where the elders sat to deal with matters brought before them (Deut. 21:19; 25:7).

The New Testament confirms the need for rebuke (Luke 17:3), particularly that official rebuke administered in the Lord's name. Writing about offenders, Paul said, "Them that sin rebuke before all" (1 Tim. 5:20). He repeated this guidance in another of his letters: "Rebuke them sharply, that they may be sound in the faith" (Titus 1:13). The minister and elders, of course, will be responsible for this censure. Thus, Timothy and Titus—who were essentially teaching elders on a special mission (that is, evangelists)—were instructed to "reprove" and "rebuke with all authority" (2 Tim. 4:2; Titus 2:15).

Acting as Christ's representatives, these rulers will base what they have to say on the Word of God. The Scriptures are specially adapted for such an end, being "profitable" for both "reproof" and "correction" (2 Tim. 3:16; see also Titus 1:9). Ministers and elders have the authority to convince men, and through divine grace, they can become the means of reclaiming men from their various sins and errors.

Since admonition is an official duty of appointed leaders in the church, they should not evidence anger, and no argument should be allowed to take place. "And the servant of the Lord," we are told, "must not strive [the Greek word means "fight" or "make war"]," but "in meekness" he should persist in "instructing those that oppose themselves" (2 Tim.

2:24–25)—that is, those who set themselves against the pure truth and good order of Christ's church.

One very important distinction should be made. If an offense was private, and perhaps minor in nature, the admonition should be delivered when the minister or elders are alone with the person who committed the offense. If, on the other hand, the offense was committed in public and was of a highly aggravated kind, the admonition should be delivered in public before the gathered church. First Timothy 5:20 instructs in particular that if an elder falls into persistent sin, admonition should take the form of "rebuke before all."

Suspension

Again, there is Old Testament precedent for this action. The ceremonial law prescribed that a person who showed symptoms of a leprous disease was to be separated from others for a certain period of time; Leviticus 13:4 directs that "the priest shall shut up him that hath the plague seven days." This was a kind of intermediate state between clean and unclean. Later that person would be examined again, and, if there was no change, it was required that "the priest shall shut him up seven days more" (v. 5).

While the children of Israel were at Hazeroth, a serious sin was committed, and the offender became subject to a real form of ecclesiastical discipline. This was the prophetess Miriam, Moses' sister. In her jealousy, she (along with Aaron) criticized Moses for marrying a Cushite woman and disputed his right to be the sole spokesman for God. The Lord was angry with Miriam and inflicted leprosy upon her. However, Moses interceded for her. As a result, she was not allowed to participate in the Lord's service, and was "shut out from the camp seven days" (Num. 12:15). That was suspension.

In the New Testament, we find Paul alluding to this censure in one of his letters. Writing to the Thessalonians, he said, "If any man obey not our word by this epistle, note that man, and have no company with him, that he may be ashamed. Yet count him not as an enemy, but admonish him as a brother" (2 Thess. 3:14–15). The discipline described in these verses falls short of that enjoined in Matthew 18:17 and elsewhere. Fellowship with this kind of person is to be restricted, but he is still to be regarded as a Christian. Furthermore, it is implied that this person will soon become ashamed, and eventually will be restored to full communion with the church.

Another passage apparently relating to this censure is Titus 3:10, in which Paul mentioned "the first and second admonition." What did he mean by these expressions? Some think this alludes to the warnings of Matthew 18:16–17; others think that private and public warnings are intended (1 Tim. 5:20; Titus 1:13), and another view is that the reference is simply to being warned once, and once again. However, there is a very strong possibility that Paul had in mind the practice of the Jewish synagogues. According to Alfred Edersheim in his magnum opus, *The Life and Times of Jesus the Messiah*, there were two stages of discipline before final excommunication. First, there was *Nezipah*, a rebuke. This rebuke was sometimes delivered during a whole day, or during a period of seven or even more days. Second, there was *Niddui*, the thrusting out. Apparently this removal from privileges lasted thirty days, and at the end of that period there was "a second admonition," delivered over a further thirty days. If the person remained impenitent, the *Cherem,* or ban, was imposed, which meant formal removal from all communion and fellowship with the professing people of God.[10]

This might well provide the key to the right understanding of Paul's words. If so, then, in the apostle's mind, the first rebuke should be followed by suspension ("the second admonition"). Paul's actual words are as follows: "A man that is an heretick after the first and second admonition reject" (Titus 3:10). If the elders find that verbal reproof has been of no avail, they should meet together and decide to proceed to the next censure. This will mean that the erring member will be denied special church privileges: for example, partaking of the sacrament, attending church meetings, and performing any Christian service. This will be for a defined period of time, during which time the minister or elders will call the person's attention to his failings and put him in mind of the need for repentance. As the Bible says, "Count him not as an enemy, but admonish him as a brother" (2 Thess. 3:15; see also Gal. 6:1). The purpose is to make the man aware of his sin. It is therefore essentially remedial, causing the man to reflect on what he has done, and so to feel deeply "ashamed" (2 Thess. 3:14).

Even when there are some good signs, the elders should not act hastily and unwisely. From the book of Leviticus we learn that even when a man was apparently cleansed of his leprosy, he had to remain outside the covenant community for a certain period of time (Lev. 14:8). The elders should lift the official censure only when there is compelling evidence of real repentance, for readmittance of an unrepentant offender

---

10. Alfred Edersheim, *The Life and Times of Jesus the Messiah* (London: Pickering & Inglis Ltd., 1883), 2:183.

will nourish hypocrisy in that individual, and bring dishonor upon the church.

Exclusion

Sadly, exclusion may sometimes prove necessary. It was well known among the Jews. According to the Levitical system, lepers were expelled from the community and were obliged to "dwell alone...without the camp" (Lev. 13:45–46; see also Num. 19:20). This was mainly for ceremonial reasons, of course, but those who were morally defiled were similarly separated from the congregation.

Ezra, who was a spiritual leader to the returned exiles, called upon the people to abandon their marriages to idolatrous, unbelieving Gentiles. A proclamation called the people to assemble at Jerusalem. It stated that any who disregarded this proclamation would be "separated from the congregation of those that had been carried away" (Ezra 10:8). Such culprits would not be allowed to attend services at the temple or take part in the offering of sacrifices for the removing of their sins. They would be totally cut off from the Jewish church.

In the New Testament system of discipline, this sanction evidently remains, for Paul wrote to the Corinthian church, "Put away from among yourselves that wicked person" (1 Cor. 5:13). Similarly, he wrote to the Galatians, saying, "I would they were even cut off which trouble you" (Gal. 5:12).

Exclusion of an individual from the church is a very solemn act. The elders will lead the church to inflict this fearful censure. Calvin wrote in his *Institutes*:

> Paul's course of action for excommunicating a man is the lawful one, provided the elders do not do it by themselves alone, but with the knowledge and approval of the

church; in this way the multitude of the people does not decide the action but observes as witness and guardian so that nothing may be done according to the whim of a few. Indeed, the whole sequence of the action, besides the calling on God's name, ought to have that gravity which bespeaks the presence of Christ in order that there may be no doubt that he himself presides at his own tribunal.[11]

God ratifies this sentence. Speaking of the church's authority to pronounce a person guilty and liable to exclusion, the Lord Jesus said: "Verily I say unto you, Whatsoever ye shall bind on earth shall be bound in heaven" (Matt. 18:18). It follows that the church should proceed most carefully in this matter, with the fear of God and with much prayer. Excommunication should not take place except in the case of extreme necessity.

When exclusion takes place according to God's Word, the member concerned forfeits all special church privileges. No longer acknowledged as a fellow Christian, he will be deprived of friendship and fellowship as well. Christ said, "Let him be unto thee as an heathen man and a publican" (Matt. 18:17). The awful consequences were described further by the apostle Paul: "I have written unto you not to keep company [with him]…with such an one no not to eat" (1 Cor. 5:11). However, excluded persons should not be forbidden to hear the preaching of God's Word. This is the only means by which they may be restored and reclaimed.

One must bear in mind that the aim of all discipline, including excommunication, is a member's repentance and reformation. It is noteworthy that the New Testament

11. Calvin, *Institutes*, 4.12.7.

mentions two cases of excommunication, and in one of them, the offender becomes a penitent and is received back into the communion of the church. This was, of course, the incestuous Corinthian, of whom Paul wrote, "Ye ought…to forgive him, and comfort him, lest perhaps such a one should be swallowed up with overmuch sorrow" (2 Cor. 2:7; see also 1 Tim. 1:19–20). It is indeed a blessed time when the Lord's people can open their arms and say to a member, "We grieved over you when you were expelled from this church. While the censure remained on you, we missed you and shed tears for you. Our hearts have been broken. Yet we have still prayed for you, longing that the Lord would grant you mercy and grace to return to Him and His people. This is a wonderful day, for God has evidently blessed His own means and restored your soul. Now our God, for His Son's sake, has forgiven you, and we therefore most heartily and gladly forgive you too. We call God to witness that we now give back to you a place among us as one of His dear people."

Maintaining a Pure Church

Church ministers and elders should recognize that, under God, they must discharge their responsibilities. Church members should submit to biblical order and support their officers in a faithful administration of church discipline. The Lord Jesus Christ must have His glory. This can occur only if the purity of the church is maintained. Without the proper exercise of authority to prevent and correct offenses, Satan will have his way, sin will proceed unchecked, and our witness and testimony will be damaged irreparably.

It is true that in this world, the church will never attain perfection. Nevertheless, we must devote all our powers to making it more worthy; and then, as a result of sound doctrine and discipline, we can look forward to that day when Christ will "present it to himself a glorious church, not having spot, or wrinkle, or any such thing," for then, at last, it will be "holy and without blemish" (Eph. 5:27).

The psalmist beautifully describes that future, blessed occasion:

> *Behold the daughter of the King*
> *All glorious is within;*
> *And with embroideries of gold*
> *Her garments wrought have been.*
>
> *She shall be brought unto the King*
> *In robes with needle wrought;*
> *Her fellow-virgins following*
> *Shall unto thee be brought.*
>
> *They shall be brought with gladness great,*
> *And mirth on ev'ry side,*
> *Into the palace of the King,*
> *And there they shall abide.*[12]

---

12. *Scottish Psalter*, 1650, Psalm 45:13–15.

CHAPTER 6

Reformed Evangelism

Ye shall receive power, after that the Holy Ghost is come upon you: and ye shall be witnesses unto me both in Jerusalem, and in all Judaea, and in Samaria, and unto the uttermost part of the earth.

—Acts 1:8

There can be no doubt that, historically, Reformed churches have had a deep passion for the souls of men and a strong desire to see the gospel spread to all the world. The long-standing Reformed focus on evangelization of the world is important to stress in these days when some appear to have lost their vision and their concern for evangelization. John Wycliffe (the Evangelical Doctor, as he was called) preached with evangelistic appeal to the people of England. As early as 1377, he sent forth his "poor priests," or itinerant preachers, "clad in russet robes of undressed wool, without sandals, purse, or scrip, a long staff in their hand, dependent for food and shelter on the good will of their neighbours, their only possession a few pages of Wycliffe's Bible."[1] Wycliffe's vision was to have a minister of the gospel in every parish, living out and teaching the faith of Christ.

---

1. H. B. Workman, *The Dawn of the Reformation* (London: Charles H. Kelly, 1901), 1:209.

In the early part of the fifteenth century, John Huss moved around Bohemia with the gospel of salvation. He preached in cities, villages, castles, fields, and forests, seeking to make God's Word known. A tribute to Huss's memory by the University of Prague in 1416 described him as a "humble man flashing with the ray of great piety...who did not refuse to bend his knees at the beds of the sick, who brought with tears the hardened to repentance...basing his appeals on the old and forgotten remedies of the Scriptures by a new and unheard of motive...showing in all things the works of love, pure faith and undeviating truth."[2]

Mention also must be made of William Tyndale, who in 1522 and 1523 commenced a gospel work in the church of St. Adeleine, at Little Sodbury, England. That building soon became too small for the huge crowds that gathered to learn the way to everlasting life. Tyndale extended his work to neighboring villages around Little Sodbury, and even to the city of Bristol, where he preached to multitudes of men and women. To a certain learned man, Tyndale once said, "If God spare my life, I will, before many years are passed, cause the boy that driveth the plough to know more of the Scriptures than you do."[3] True to his word, Tyndale published his English version of the New Testament in 1525.

John Calvin, the greatest of the Reformers, once declared that he would willingly cross seven seas to bring the gospel to one needy sinner. In 1556, Calvin sent Richier, Chartier, and twelve

---

2. Victor Budgen, *On Fire for God: The Story of John Huss* (Darlington, U.K.: Evangelical Press, 1983), 85.

3. R. Demaus, *William Tyndale, a Biography* (London: Religious Tract Society, 1886), 72–73.

others to take the Word of Life to Brazil. Tragically, five of those men were put to death, and the rest had to return to Europe.

Calvin nevertheless continued to be concerned for the spread of the gospel. In Calvin's Geneva, men were taught God's way of salvation that they might in turn teach it to others, and many did. According to contemporary records, between 1555 and 1562, no fewer than eighty-eight men were sent out to various parts of the world—and these records are far from complete. We know from other sources, for example, that in the single year of 1561 alone, 142 men left Geneva to engage in missionary activity.[4]

The following century saw the departure of the Pilgrims for New England. They lost no time in evangelizing the Indians. As early as 1621, one of their number was set apart to preach the gospel to them. In 1646, John Eliot began gospel work in a small Indian village near Watertown. At the same time, Thomas Mayhew and his son were seeking to win to Christ the Indians on some of the islands near Boston. By 1674, there were said to be about four thousand converted Indians in New England.

In 1649, the English Parliament passed an ordinance that created the first Protestant missionary society. It was called the Corporation for the Propagation of the Gospel in New England. Reformed churches took up a general collection for it, as did Cromwell's army, and twelve thousand pounds was raised to support this evangelistic work.

In 1647, the General Assembly of the Church of Scotland recorded its desire for "a more firm consociation for

---

4. Philip E. Hughes, "John Calvin: Director of Missions," in *The Heritage of John Calvin*, ed. John H. Bratt (Grand Rapids: Eerdmans, 1973), 46.

propagating [the gospel] to those who are without."[5] As a consequence, in 1670 certain ministers were sent out by the Assembly to take God's truth to those without it.

The name of William Carey must also be included here. In 1792, he published his *Enquiry into the Obligations of Christians to Use Means for the Conversion of the Heathen*. That very year saw the formation of the Particular Baptist Society for the Propagation of the Gospel amongst the Heathen. (In the society's name, *Particular* indicated it was Calvinistic.) It was founded with funds amounting to 13.25 pounds. Carey himself sailed for India in the year 1793.

Christ, the Greatest Evangelist

The Bible teaches that the Son of God was the greatest evangelist of all time. Old Testament prophecy referred to Him as "a light to the Gentiles" and God's "salvation unto the end of the earth" (Isa. 49:6). The same prophetic book represents the Lord Jesus as speaking in this way: "The spirit of the Lord GOD is upon me; because the LORD hath anointed me to preach good tidings unto the meek" (61:1). In another place He is heard, as "the wisdom of God," preaching the gospel in a most public and earnest manner: "Unto you, O men, I call; and my voice is to the sons of man. O ye simple, understand wisdom: and, ye fools, be ye of an understanding heart. Hear; for I will speak of excellent things; and the opening of my lips shall be right things" (Prov. 8:4–6). Thomas Goodwin, the Puritan, once said: "God had but one Son, and he made him a minister."[6]

---

5. George Smith, *Short History of Christian Missions* (Edinburgh: Morrison & Gibb, 1904), 133.

6. Thomas Goodwin, *Works of Thomas Goodwin* (Edinburgh: James Nichol, 1863), 6:415.

Christ Himself indicated that His mission was "to seek and to save that which was lost" (Luke 19:10). He preached the gospel publicly in the open air, in people's homes, and in the synagogues. Privately, He taught individuals such as Nicodemus and Zacchaeus. Looking beyond the Jewish people to whom He was first sent, Christ spoke of the worldwide scope of the gospel. He made special mention of "other sheep" which were "not of this fold" (that is, not found within Judaism): "Them also I must bring," He said, "and there shall be one fold, and one shepherd" (John 10:16). In fact, He spoke graciously to the woman of Canaan, commended the faith of the centurion, and taught and healed those who came to Him from Decapolis, Idumaea, and from beyond Jordan. Our Lord made very clear to His disciples that before long His evangelistic ministry would be transferred to them. In the Sermon on the Mount, Christ, who is Himself "the light of the world," described His disciples with that phrase (Matt. 5:14). No doubt that was one of the reasons our Lord chose to have His disciples with Him while He was involved in mission. They were trainees, not only learning for themselves the great truths of God, but also learning how to present these truths to others.

The Church's Commission

At the time of His ascension, the Lord Jesus formally transferred His evangelistic function to the Christian church. "Go ye therefore," He said, "and teach all nations" (Matt. 28:19; see also Mark 16:15). According to Luke's gospel, He told them that "repentance and remission of sins should be preached in his name among all nations, beginning at Jerusalem" (Luke 24:47). Accordingly, the early church brought the gospel to Jerusalem (Acts 2–7), Judaea and Samaria (8–9:31), and the uttermost parts of the earth (10–28). The apostles understood that the church was continuing Christ's work. One of the great concepts in Paul's epistles is that of the church as "[Christ's] body" (Eph. 1:23). One theologian put it like this: "As in his incarnate life, Christ had to have a body to proclaim his Gospel and to do his work, so in his resurrection life in this age he still needs a body to be the instrument of his Gospel and of his work in the world."[7] So the church represents Christ's interests in this world, and is to carry on His work of evangelizing its peoples. Indeed, this is the task of each instituted and organized local church.

In his first letter to Timothy, Paul expressed the hope that he would soon be able to visit Ephesus, but he added that he had written his letter to instruct Timothy how to act in "the church of the living God, the pillar and ground [or support] of the truth" (1 Tim. 3:15). The idea here is that a church is meant to uphold, or bear aloft, the truth, so that people all over the region may be confronted with it. Of course, that should be true of every local church. Ministers, in particular, have the responsibility of preaching the gospel (2 Tim. 4:2), but individual Christians or members are told, "Be ready always to give an answer to every man that asketh you a reason of the hope that is in you" (1 Peter 3:15).

"Go Out!"

Our God-given mandate is to move out into the world. The Lord Jesus said in His Commission: "Go ye into all the world" (Mark 16:15). In the parable of the great supper recorded in

---

7. Alan Richardson, *An Introduction to the Theology of the New Testament* (London: SCM Press, 1966), 256.

Luke 14:16–24, He likened His disciples to servants who had been "sent," and twice in that parable these servants were told to "go." "Go out quickly into the streets and lanes of the city.... Go out into the highways and hedges." In this connection, we should remember the words of our Lord about the vine and its branches. He was speaking of the need for fruitfulness and He said, "Ye have not chosen me, but I have chosen you, and ordained you, that ye should go and bring forth fruit" (John 15:16).

The church must never lose its sense of calling. As the Lord's people, we are not to remain within the walls of our buildings, comforting ourselves with the Scriptures and glorying in the doctrines of grace. We must always be mindful of the fact that outside, there are thousands of Christless and hopeless souls. Surely, we have a responsibility to tell them of God's salvation. What could we do? We could hold open-air services. We could distribute Christian tracts. We could gather children for Christian instruction. We could use all lawful means to save the lost. A church that ceases to evangelize is not obedient to God's Word, and it is certainly not Reformed.

The Church Must Grow

Writing to the church at Thessalonica, the apostle Paul told them that he was very glad to hear of the church's evangelistic work. "For from you," he said, "sounded out the word of the Lord not only in Macedonia and Achaia, but also in every place your faith to God-ward is spread abroad; so that we need not to speak any thing" (1 Thess. 1:8). If only this were true of every Reformed church today! Of the early Christians it was said that they had "filled Jerusalem with their doctrine." If we are their successors, we will surely fill our cities with the good news of Jesus Christ. This is the only way for the church to grow—and the Lord *does* will that His church should grow.

Some Christians appear to think that it is a virtue to be incredibly small, to be in a state of decline, to be just a chosen few. However, our Lord tells us very clearly that He intends to enlarge His church: "I will build my church; and the gates of hell shall not prevail against it" (Matt. 16:18). In the parable mentioned above, the servants are sent out, and still there is room. So they are sent out again, and again. Our Lord's last words to them in the parable are, "Go out into the highways and hedges, and compel them to come in, *that my house may be filled*" (Luke 14:23, italics added). The book of Acts also makes clear that God is concerned with the increase of numbers. Time and again, particularly in the early chapters, we read how the Lord added to the church. He added more, even thousands, to the number of believers. Indeed, He "added to the church daily such as should be saved" (Acts 2:47).

According to Romans 11, there is such a thing as the "fulness" of the Gentiles, that great number of God's elect gathered from the nations before the conversion of the Jews; and there is also such a thing as the "fulness" of Israel, that vast multitude of Jews comprehended in God's saving purposes. The very term suggests that a great many souls are to be brought to Christ and into His church. When Jesus sent out seventy apostles (Luke 10:1), it is said that upon their return from their preaching mission, the Lord "rejoiced in spirit" (v. 21). What was it that made Him so glad? It was the report they brought him of gospel success. Sinners were turning to the Savior, and they were being delivered from the power of evil. His kingdom was coming in power. Its boundaries were being extended. The church was growing, to our Lord's glory and praise. It is the grand vision of the Reformed faith to see the gospel taken to the ends of the earth, the Scriptures published in every language, and sinners gathered to Christ from every kindred, tongue, people, and nation.

Light and Heat

If we are in union with Christ, gospel success will please us too. Grieved over the church's failure and barrenness, we will pray, as Christians, for her prosperity, and we will be so thankful to know that our prayers are being answered. To see the church flourish in this world is one of our greatest spiritual delights. Be assured that there is no incompatibility between doctrinal orthodoxy and compassion for the souls of men and women. These things are inseparable.

Some people have all "light" in their religion. They can recite large sections of the confession and the larger and shorter catechisms—and, no doubt, a great deal more besides. Yet it seems to be all "light." True Reformed Christianity is "light" and "heat." It is fire. The "light" of knowledge is attended with the "heat" of holy concern and of passion for the salvation of sinners. You can feel the "heat" in Paul's words to the church at Rome: "I say the truth in Christ, I lie not, my conscience also bearing me witness in the Holy Ghost, that I have great heaviness and continual sorrow in my heart. For I could wish that myself were accursed from Christ for my brethren, my kinsmen according to the flesh" (Rom. 9:1–3). In another place he wrote as follows: "Brethren, my heart's desire and prayer to God for Israel is, that they might be saved" (Rom. 10:1). Now, this is apostolic religion. The heart is engaged, emotions are stirred, and eyes are overflowing with tears. This is the religion that moves us in the direction of unbelievers, to use all lawful means to snatch them as brands from the burning. Where real Christianity is in evidence, Christ's blessed presence will be felt and known. He promises His presence to the evangelizing church.

Christ's Presence Known

Let the words of Christ's Great Commission always challenge you: "Go ye therefore, and teach all nations, baptizing them in the name of the Father, and of the Son, and of the Holy Ghost." Then come these precious words: "And, lo, I am with you always [literally, all the days], even unto the end of the world" (Matt. 28:19–20). The Lord graciously fulfilled His promise, to the great comfort and encouragement of His obedient disciples. According to Mark's gospel, they went out into the world with the Word of Life, "the Lord working with them, and confirming the word with signs following" (Mark 16:20). Later, Paul was able to make mention of his own evangelistic experience. He wrote of himself and others as being "labourers together with God" (1 Cor. 3:9; see also 2 Cor. 6:1). The fact is that those who engage in this great work will know the Lord's presence. A church obedient to the Great Commission is a church with Jesus Christ in the midst. Alexander Duff of the Free Church of Scotland once said, "What is the whole history of the Christian Church, but one perpetual proof and illustration of the grand position—that an evangelistic or missionary church is a spiritually flourishing church; and, that a church which drops the evangelistic or missionary character, speedily lapses into superannuation and decay!"[8]

---

8. Alexander Duff, *Missions: The Chief End of the Christian Church* (Edinburgh: J. Johnstone, 1839), 15.

A church that seeks to win precious souls will be divinely approved and commended. John the Baptist was said to be "great in the sight of the Lord." Why exactly was that? One of the reasons is given in Scripture: "And many of the children of Israel shall he turn to the Lord their God" (Luke 1:15–16). Something similar is said about Barnabas: "He was a good man, and full of the Holy Ghost and of faith." What did he do to deserve such honor? Read what immediately follows: "And much people was added unto the Lord" (Acts 11:24).

The soul-winner's greatest reward will be in the future: "And they that be wise shall shine as the brightness of the firmament; and they that turn many to righteousness as the stars for ever and ever" (Dan. 12:3). Writing to the Thessalonians, Paul, the great evangelist, said, "For what is our hope, or joy, or crown of rejoicing? Are not even ye in the presence of our Lord Jesus Christ at his coming?" (1 Thess. 2:19). The apostle was greatly looking forward to that day when he will be brought before the Son of God, with the knowledge that he will not then appear alone. All his dear converts will be there with him. What enhancement of his joy when he sees them all around him! How much more glorious the crown of his reward when he leads them forward to the throne! It is not for us to anticipate meeting the Lord Jesus on that day without the knowledge that we have been instrumental in bringing others to Him.

The Message for Sinners

The church's message, of course, is the gospel. This gospel contains doctrinal statements about God's wonderful love, His purpose to save sinners, His appointment of His Son as their Redeemer; the necessity of union with Him, and the resultant justification unto life. The gospel also contains precious promises of salvation, sincere offers of mercy, and pressing invitations to believe on the Lord Jesus Christ. This gospel must be taught by word of mouth. This can be done publicly in preaching, as the open proclamation of God's truth in this world (Rom. 10:15; 1 Cor. 1:21). It can also be done privately, as the testimony or witness of one to another (Acts 18:26; 22:12–16). No matter how it is verbally communicated, there is need of the Holy Spirit to quicken those dead in their sins, awaken them to their danger as condemned sinners, and constrain them to believe with all their hearts in Jesus Christ, their only hope in time and in eternity. How much confusion there seems to be today concerning this message! We will examine it in more depth.

Plain Declaration

Scripture requires a clear, verbal, and systematic declaration of the gospel, not the clever use of various gimmicks. The preacher should ensure that the message is not mixed with worthless and injurious extras. As the apostle says, "We are not as many, which corrupt the word of God" (2 Cor. 2:17). That word *corrupt* designates the business of a wine merchant who is accustomed to mingle water with his wine (Isa. 1:22). We should not dilute the pure Word of God with such trappings as testimonies, musical solos, or dramatic performances. We must not use devices to trick people, as if we are dishonest and ingratiating salesmen. Instead, we must present the saving facts concerning Christ crucified, risen, and now reigning in glory. "[We] have renounced the hidden things of dishonesty, not walking in craftiness, nor handling the word of God deceitfully; but by manifestation of the truth commending ourselves to every man's conscience in the sight of God" (2 Cor. 4:2).

True evangelistic preaching, therefore, is instructive, not entertaining. "[Christ] we preach," said Paul, "warning every man, and teaching every man in all wisdom" (Col. 1:28). Our mandate is to deal with sin. It is to expose the sinner's need. It is to warn of the dreadful and eternal consequences of offending God. Then it is to open up the revealed truths concerning the Savior, setting forth His Godhood and His manhood; His offices of prophet, priest, and king; and His work of atonement in covering our offenses by adequate compensation. It is to proclaim Christ as the sole refuge for weak and helpless sinners. It is to call sinners to flee from the storm of divine judgment and to find their shelter in the Savior's protecting love. It is to assure everyone who truly believes of pardon, peace, and eternal security. *This* is our gospel, and to present it faithfully is to "fulfil the word of God" (Col. 1:25; see also Rom. 15:19).

God at the Center

In preaching the gospel it is important not to concentrate on man. Modern evangelism tends to promote the evangelist as the one who is well worth listening to. His name, ability, and successes are brought to the fore as a means of attracting people's attention and their presence at meetings. Advertisements everywhere will carry the evangelist's picture and record his previous crusades. It is all very much taken up with the evangelist himself. Very different indeed was the approach of the apostle Paul, who once said, "Not that we are sufficient of ourselves to think any thing as of ourselves" (2 Cor. 3:5). If the great nineteenth-century preacher Asahel Nettleton sensed that churches were relying on him in any way, he would resolutely refuse to accept their invitations to preach among them. He believed that there would be no blessing if people were looking to him rather than to the Lord.

Of course, not every preacher is like Nettleton. Some seem intent on drawing attention to themselves. I once listened to a tape of an evangelist preaching in London. This man preached for about thirty-five minutes, and I would estimate that 75 percent of the sermon was about himself. He told his hearers where he had been, how many people had gathered to hear him, and what the results had been in various parts of the world. It was very hard to listen to this man's preaching (if that is the right name for it). When the sermon was over, I wished I could have spoken to him, just to say, "We preach not ourselves, but Christ Jesus the Lord" (2 Cor. 4:5).

After hearing a certain Dr. Elmslie preach, someone wrote the following lines:

> *He held the lamp of Truth that day*
> *So low that none could miss the way*
> *And yet so high to bring in sight*
> *That picture fair, the world's great light,*
> *That, gazing up—the lamp between*
> *The hand that held it scarce was seen.*
>
> *He held the pitcher, stooping low,*
> *To lips of little ones below,*
> *Then raised it to the weary saint*
> *And bade him drink when sick and faint.*
> *They drank—the pitcher thus between*
> *The hand that held it scarce was seen.*
>
> *He blew the trumpet soft and clear,*
> *That trembling sinners need not fear,*
> *And then with louder note and bold,*
> *To raze the walls of Satan's hold.*

The trumpet coming thus between
The hand that held it scarce was seen!

But when the Captain says "Well done,
Thou good and faithful servant, Come!
Lay down the trumpet, leave the Camp,"
The weary hands will then be seen,
Clasped in those pierced ones, naught between.[9]

Our message must be God-centered in every way. There are those who carefully avoid the excesses to which we have just referred, yet they preach all about man, his needs and his desires. They put questions like these to the congregation: What is it that you want? Is it joy and peace? Is it satisfaction for your heart? Is it a purpose for life? Is it a sense of real security? They may offer literature at the end of meetings to answer these very questions. This is *not* the Christian message. The Christian message is not about man; it is about God.

The truth is, God made us in order that we may worship and serve Him, and live to His glory. Sin can only be explained in terms of rebellion against Him, and as breach of His holy and just law. In His great mercy, however, He planned and provided salvation in His Son, to deliver sinners from sin's dreadful punishment. God has opened wide the door of His mercy, calling one and all to turn to the blessed Savior for a divine, full, free, present, and everlasting salvation. God commands—He entreats—He beseeches the poor lost souls of men and women: Why, O why, will they die? God's heart is towards them. His desires are towards them. His interest in

---

9. Harold Murray, *Dinsdale Young* (London: Marshall, Morgan & Scott, 1938), 142–43.

their welfare is as sincere as it is deep. God is willing to save every believer in the Lord Jesus Christ.

Furthermore, He has prepared a heaven for the saved (as well as a hell for the lost). Believers can look forward to more than the shadows of this vain world. Their God will be their portion forever. This is the gospel, the gospel of God. It always was the gospel, and it always will be the gospel. Salvation is of the Lord! It begins, proceeds, and ends in God. Wicked, hell-deserving sinners need to be shown that there is a God with whom they have to do; a God who has so loved the world that He has given His only begotten Son; and a God who will one day welcome chosen, redeemed, and called sinners into His eternal kingdom. These are the grand verities that constitute the gospel of our salvation, and these are the verities that must be preached to all people in every part of this world.

Conviction of Sin

All too often today, an evangelist will emphasize the problems of unemployment, economic disparities, the violations of human rights, natural disasters, and so on. These are general references to the present state of this poor world. What is really needed is "law-work," the exposition and application of the law to the consciences of sinners. As "the spirit of bondage," the Holy Spirit uses the law to convince of sin and misery (John 16:8; Rom. 8:15). He enforces the law's commands, as Paul found in his own experience: "For I was alive without the law once: but when the commandment came, sin revived, and I died" (Rom. 7:9). In other words, there was a time when Paul, as a proud Pharisee, thought himself blameless before God. Then the law was brought home to him in its authority and in the extent and spirituality of its commands. At once, he saw in his heart and life a multitude of sins of which he had hitherto been completely unaware. Sin revived; that is, it seemed to appear everywhere, and, as never before, he became deeply conscious of original and actual sin. He died, as it were. He felt condemned, without any hope at all. In this state of misery, he could only cry out, "O wretched man that I am! who shall deliver me from the body of this death?" It was then, and only then, that he was ready to desire Christ as his sole helper. "Who shall deliver me...? I thank God [who has provided salvation] through Jesus Christ our Lord" (Rom. 7:24–25).

The Spirit not only enforces the law's commands; He also confirms the law's *curses*. We return to Paul's words in Romans 7. "And the commandment," he says, "which was ordained to life, I found to be unto death" (v. 10). Obedience to God's commands was originally designed to be the condition of life in the covenant of works. Paul, under the Spirit's teaching, had become conscious of the number and power of his sins, and the law now seemed only to threaten death to him as a transgressor. To the guilty sinner, the law is indeed "the ministration of death" (2 Cor. 3:7). That is what the Holy Spirit does to the elect sinner. He convinces us of sin and of misery. When the Spirit attended the preaching of God's Word on the day of Pentecost, those who heard that preaching realized that they had committed an awful crime and that consequently their souls were in real danger, and they were "pricked in their heart." They cried out to Peter and the others, "Men and brethren, what shall we do?" (Acts 2:37).

Many preachers today seem unaware of the necessity of this "law-work." Yet if they do not preach the law in such a way that their hearers are deeply affected by it, the result will be many spurious conversions and many deluded hypocrites in our churches. In one of his sermons, Martin Luther said, "Moses must always go before, who may teach us to feel sin, whereby grace may be wished for and desired of us; it is vain, therefore, although Christ be preached to be loving, and to be desired and longed for, if a man be not before humbled through knowledge of himself."[10]

Mind, Heart, and Will

The gospel must be addressed to the whole person. It must (with the power of the Spirit) inform the mind, move the heart, and then bend the will. It is all too easy for the preacher to concentrate upon one of these, to the neglect or total exclusion of the others. For example, a sermon can be full of sound doctrine, but it is sadly possible for people to understand divine things but, spiritually speaking, be none the better for it. So, some are merely "enlightened" and lacking other "things that accompany salvation" (Heb. 6:4–9). Under such preaching, it is possible to understand the truths of the faith, and even to understand the truths concerning the Son of God—"the knowledge of the Lord and Saviour Jesus Christ"—and yet not to be converted, but still to be ensnared by "the pollutions of the world" (2 Peter 2:20). This is a mere "form of knowledge" (Rom. 2:20).

In another way, it is possible for the preacher to place too much stress on feelings. He may influence people by speaking smoothly to them: "They have seduced my people, saying, Peace" (Ezek. 13:10; see also Jer. 6:14; 8:11). Some are easily affected by this kind of teaching, and they can be carried

---

10. Martin Luther, *Sermons by Martin Luther*, ed. James Kerr (Edinburgh: Lyon & Gemmell, 1875), 115–16.

away by it, like those whom Paul calls "children" and "silly women" (Eph. 4:14; 2 Tim. 3:6). This is a matter of great concern because the result is often only an emotional response. Did not the Lord warn of this danger in the parable of the sower? Some receive the truth "with joy," yet they are soon found to have no "root" in themselves. That is, they are superficial, without any depth of conviction (Matt. 13:20–21).

Again, like the scribes and Pharisees, the preacher may be so keen to win converts (Matt. 23:15) that he puts great pressure on people to make immediate "decisions." Time will show, however, that many of these supposed conversions are completely spurious. In the parable of the two sons, the father said to one of them, "Son, go work today in my vineyard," and right away the boy answered, "I go." In the event, however, he did not go at all (Matt. 21:28–30). This son represents people who make decisions but then fail to deliver. If there is concentration upon a person's will, there may be some kind of resolution to obey the Word and enter the church of God. But a fair promise does not, in and of itself, make someone a true Christian. Conversion is not just a matter of the will.

The gospel must reach the whole person; the mind must be informed, the heart must be stirred, and then the will must be taken. This is the apostolic way. According to the book of Acts, in Rome Paul "expounded [the mind] and testified the kingdom of God [the heart], persuading them concerning Jesus [the will], both out of the law of Moses, and out of the prophets, from morning till evening" (Acts 28:23).

Salvation from Sin
Gospel preaching must explain salvation, and should do so strictly in terms of salvation from sin. All too often, preachers

represent salvation as some kind of insurance policy, to keep people out of hell. Such sermons usually conclude like this: "If you died this very night, where would your soul go? Where will your soul be throughout eternity?" Of course, the average person does not want to end up in the regions of the damned. He or she would much rather experience everlasting happiness with the blessed. It is therefore quite possible to move people to the point that they are able to say, with Balaam, "Let me die the death of the righteous, and let my last end be like his!" (Num. 23:10). Yet, remember: We have every reason to believe that the man who uttered those words lived impenitently and then perished in his sin. A "gospel" that produces only that kind of response is inherently defective.

Salvation, according to the Bible, rescues us from sin's power as well as from its penalty. As the angel said to Joseph concerning the Lord Jesus, "Thou shalt call his name JESUS: for he shall *save his people from their sins*" (Matt. 1:21, italics added). Again, Christ is said to have given Himself for us, "that he might *redeem us from all iniquity*, and purify unto himself a peculiar people, zealous of good works" (Titus 2:14).

You may be familiar with the account of Augustine. Advised by Ambrose to read Paul's letters, Augustine read the letter to the Romans. After reading the first chapter, he really felt he could read no more, so concerned and distressed was he about the condition of his sinful and wretched soul. He ran away from the place where he had been reading, but suddenly he heard the voices of children, "Take up and read! Take up and read!" Believing that God was speaking to him through their voices, he returned to where he had previously been. Taking up the book, he read this time the words: "not in revelling and drunkenness, not in lust and wantonness, not in

quarrels and rivalries. Rather, arm yourselves with the Lord
Jesus Christ; spend no more thought on nature and nature's
appetites" (Rom. 13:13–15). Augustine saw that his greatest
problem was sin, and that only the Lord Jesus Christ could
deliver him from that sin. This led him to turn to the Savior
and to cast his sinful soul upon Him for full salvation.[11]

As Ralph Erskine preached:

> Christ…is not offered as a Saviour only, to save from hell;
> but as a Lord also to deliver from sin. Now what is the
> great obstruction here, that hinders the receiving of the
> offer? Why, it is even the false heart that would divide
> salvation from dominion; would be content to have his
> soul saved, but not to have the sin conquered, would have
> Christ as a Jesus, but not as a Lord; the man would be
> under his garment, and yet not under his government. In
> this case the man is not so much out of love with sin, as
> out of love with hell; not so much in love with Christ, as
> with his benefits: while his guilt craves Christ's salvation,
> his lusts oppose Christ's Lordship.[12]

Correct Terminology

Preachers should take great care to use words and phrases
sanctioned by the Scriptures, rather than inadequate modern
equivalents that often obscure the truth. Take, for example,
a word commonly used today in preaching and teaching,
the word *commitment*. In general use, it refers to the sense of
attachment or engagement. We often hear it from the pulpit in

---

11. Saint Augustine, *Confessions* (New York: Penguin Books, 1961),
177–78.

12. Ralph Erskine, *The Sermons and Other Practical Works of the Rev-
erend and Learned Ralph Erskine* (London: R. Baynes, 1821), 3:15.

phrases such as "Commit yourself to the Lord Jesus Christ." However, in the Bible, the word *commitment* does not mean a loving response to the Lord. It translates a word that literally means a "deposit." It refers to the fact that the believer has "entrusted" his soul to the one and only Savior of sinners, the Lord Jesus Christ. The apostle Paul wrote, "He is able to keep that which I have committed unto him against that day" (2 Tim. 1:12). Luther paraphrased that verse with these words: "Let him who died for my soul see to the salvation of it."[13] The problem of using *commitment* in the modern sense is that the sinner's response becomes one of promise, rather than one of trust.

A similar objection can be made to the words *accept* and *acceptance*. It is common to hear people speak of "accepting the Lord Jesus as a personal savior." Now, that is not a Bible word; in the Bible, we read of "receiving" Christ Jesus the Lord. There is a subtle but important difference. A voter can accept a political candidate, and a woman may accept the overtures of her lover. However, subjects are not asked to accept their sovereign.

It is necessary, in these days, to hold on to biblical expressions. You may say, "The problem is that people just don't understand these expressions." My reply to that is the minister's responsibility is to explain these words and concepts so that people will be able to understand.

Free Grace

The emphasis should always be upon grace—the sovereign, matchless, and distinguishing grace of God. The nineteenth-century British Baptist preacher Charles Spurgeon memorably

---

13. Martin Luther, quoted by Thomas Brooks, in *Works of Thomas Brooks*, ed. Alexander B. Grosart (Edinburgh: Banner of Truth, 1980), 3:198.

said that some preachers had an impediment in their speech. In their sermons, they meant to say free grace, but it always seemed to come out as free will!

Warfield once wrote, "Evangelical religion reaches its full manifestation…only when the sinful soul rests in humble, self-emptying trust purely on the God of grace as the immediate and sole source of all the efficiency which enters into its salvation."[14]

The gospel should be so preached that grace will saturate the entire message. Grace, from all eternity, determined that there would be a salvation for sinners. Grace moved God to choose some sinners of mankind to be the recipients of that salvation. Grace was responsible for the drawing up of salvation's plan (the covenant of grace). Grace, in the fullness of time, sent Christ to accomplish the divine salvation. Grace ordered the preaching of the gospel of salvation to the ends of the earth. Grace ensures the bestowal of the Spirit, to convict men of sin, to bring them to Jesus Christ, and to put them in possession of this great salvation. Furthermore, grace will keep them to the end, and grace will finally lead them into the glory of the eternal kingdom. It is grace from beginning to end. It is altogether and only of grace. It is salvation by grace, the real, pure, and rich grace of God. And when the multitude of the elect, perfected in their bodies and souls, enter the everlasting glory, they will exclaim, with adoring praises, "Grace, grace unto it" (Zech. 4:7). That sound will never die away.

The Need for Compassion
How moving those words are, recorded in Luke 19:41: "And when he was come near, he beheld the city, and wept over it."

---

14. Warfield, *Calvin as a Theologian and Calvinism Today*, 16.

Our dear Savior wept! At the grave of Lazarus He wept, but a different word is used here. There "He shed silent tears," but here "He wept aloud, bewailing."[15] What follows shows that He was so choked with emotion that He could hardly speak. The words could be rendered like this: "If thou hadst known in this day—even thou—the things that belong unto peace! but now they are hid from thine eyes." These are broken sentences, showing the intensity of His sorrow. Language seems to fail Him. The sense is there, but it is not properly expressed. His anguish and grief are too great for ordinary words. In that moment, the human language seemed woefully inadequate. His words foundered on nothing less than the rock of His immense love.

Here was love beyond degree! In the next few days, He would endure great insults and sorrows in the garden, in the judgment hall, and at the place called Golgotha. But He would never feel or speak as He did on this occasion. His deepest concerns were not for Himself but for unbelieving sinners. Our Lord wept over Jerusalem because He knew the worth of their souls. He knew that sin would one day be their ruin, yet He beheld the people of Jerusalem despising the mercy offered to them in the gospel. He wept because He really cared for them. He could hardly bear to contemplate their future plight, and He yearned, as no other ever did, for their spiritual deliverance. He wept because He knew that, in spite of their blessings, they were in danger of being eternally lost. They had received the oracles of God, the ministry of prophets, and the wonderful blessings of God—but all to no account, for they faced a hopeless existence in the next world. He wept

---

15. Author's translation from the original.

because their excuses were feeble and would prove to be of no avail on the great day of judgment. In the final analysis, they would perish on account of their own impenitence and unbelief. He wept because He was only too aware of the doom that now awaited them. His heart broke as He foresaw God's overwhelming wrath, the unquenchable fire of hell, and the never-ending pain and torment. He wept!

Something of that love must be in our hearts. As we look out on a world in revolt against God, in breach of His holy law, in the way of His judgment, we surely cannot be indifferent or unmoved. You and I, my friends, have the gospel, which alone affords hope to transgressors. We have proved in our own experience that Christ is able, willing, and ready to save. We have His wonderful example, the indwelling of His Holy Spirit, and the love of God shed abroad in our hearts. That love constrains us! It constrains us to feel concern, to pray for poor sinners, and to tell them of the Savior we have found.

The church's task is to preach God's Word. The church's message is salvation through grace alone and by faith alone. The church's compassion is Christ's love in our hearts, flowing out to the lost. God grant us grace to proclaim to our generation the glorious gospel of the Protestant Reformation!

CHAPTER 7

Maintaining the Reformed Faith

But they are not valiant for the truth upon the earth; for they proceed from evil to evil, and they know not me, saith the LORD.

—Jeremiah 9:3

In the prophet Jeremiah's day, the church was in a desperate condition. The people had been unfaithful to God, and towards their fellow men they were deceitful and malicious, totally corrupt in their varied dealings, "an assembly of treacherous men." Jeremiah deplored the fact that no one seemed to be "valiant for the truth upon the earth." How similar his days seem to ours. We, too, need to strive to be men and women who are "valiant for the truth."

In *The Pilgrim's Progress,* Bunyan characterized a man valiant for the truth, fervent in spirit, and full of faith:

[He stood] with his sword drawn, and his face all bloody. Then said Mr. Great-heart, What art thou?

The man made answer, saying, I am one whose name is Valiant-for-truth. I am a pilgrim, and am going to the Celestial City. Now, as I was in my way, there were three men did beset me…. Then these three, to wit, Wild-head, Inconsiderate and Pragmatic, drew upon me, and I also drew upon them. So we fell to it, one against three, for the space of above three hours. They have left upon me, as you see, some of the marks of their valour, and have also carried away with them some of mine....

But here was great odds [said Mr. Great-heart], three against one.

It is true [answered Valiant]; but little and more are nothing to him that has the truth on his side. "Though an host should encamp against me, said one, my heart shall not fear: though war should rise against me, in this *will* I *be* confident" (Ps. 27:3).[1]

There is much we can learn from a consideration of the amazing truth we possess, and the battle that is constantly being waged for it.

Being Courageous for the Truth

We can only become brave and courageous for the truth when we have a true knowledge of God and a profound sense of His glory. According to Solomon, "In the fear of the LORD is strong confidence" (Prov. 14:26). A person who is profoundly aware of God and His almighty presence will not dread even the strongest enemy or the worst adversity. "If God be for us, who can be against us?" (Rom. 8:31). In the book of Acts, after Peter and John had spent time with the Lord Jesus, they appeared before the Sanhedrin. Although they were threatened, they evidenced tremendous bravery, "transforming the prisoner's bar into a pulpit from which to preach a gospel sermon."[2] The members of the Sanhedrin saw "the boldness

---

1. Bunyan, *The Pilgrim's Progress*, in *Works*, 3:232–33.
2. Thomas Whitelaw, *The Preacher's Complete Homiletic Commentary on the Acts of the Apostles* (New York: Funk & Wagnalls, 1896), 106.

of Peter and John," and "they took knowledge of them, that they had been with Jesus" (Acts 4:13).

What are we to be valiant for? "Valiant for the truth," says Jeremiah. Now, we understand *truth* here to be a synonym for the Word of God. Remember how the Lord Jesus, in John 17, said, "Thy word is truth" (v. 17). What cause we have to stand firm for truth such as this! There is nothing we can rely on so completely and utterly as the Word of God. We have the truth in writing from God; He is its author, and He can never lie. It is truth without any mixture of error, like silver tried in a furnace of earth, "purified seven times" (Ps. 12:6), and it encompasses the fullness of divine revelation. Whatever truths God has revealed through nature (as taught in Ps. 19:1; Acts 14:15; Rom. 1:19–20) inevitably prove incomplete and inadequate, particularly in the matter of the way of salvation. The Bible, on the other hand, is full, containing everything we need to get to heaven. In its holy pages we are confronted with "all truth" (John 16:13), to which nothing should be added, neither by way of further revelation nor by ecclesiastical tradition.

The Power of Truth

The truth of Scripture is also demonstrated by its great power over the hearts of men, both to convert and to sanctify. In this world, there is nothing more persuasive or compelling than the declaration of the truth. The apostle Paul spoke of the truth as "mighty through God" (2 Cor. 10:4) and that which "effectually worketh" (1 Thess. 2:13). The truth illuminates the benighted mind, softens the resistant heart, and ultimately captures the citadel of the will. "And ye shall know the truth," Christ once said, "and the truth shall make you free" (John 8:32). This truth will never change. No matter what theories are devised, no matter what philosophies are propounded, this grand old Book will not be disproved nor will it be shaken: "For ever, O LORD, thy word is settled in heaven" (Ps. 119:89). Truth is unchangeably fixed, as firm and immovable as Jehovah's throne.

The truth is absolutely faithful and trustworthy. Its every promise will be fulfilled, and its every threat will be realized. "God is not a man, that he should lie; neither the son of man, that he should repent: hath he said, and shall he not do it? or hath he spoken, and shall he not make it good?" (Num. 23:19). We are not dealing here with fiction or fable. We are dealing with truth. Here, in our hands, is a volume of verities and certainties. Men's words can never be trusted because their minds are darkened. Hence, their ideas, systems, and philosophies are riddled with misconceptions and falsehoods. But the God who cannot lie has caused His Word to be written down in the Holy Scriptures. Here we have something more excellent than anything human. "All scripture is given by inspiration of God." This is the truth. Oh, that we might know something of the power of it!

Three Forms of Truth

There is, first of all, natural truth. In viewing creation and providence, we may be able to discern a divine hand at work. This takes us some way in knowledge but by no means far enough. Natural revelation fails to make known the plan of redemption; it does not exhibit the Son of God as an all-sufficient savior, and it does not guide sinners into the way of sins forgiven, peace with God, and hope of heaven.

Secondly, there is legal truth. More knowledge is made available through the law. The apostle Paul confirmed this in Romans 2 when he said that the Jews had "the form of knowledge and of the truth in the law" (Rom. 2:20). In the law, we may learn something of God's holiness, justice, and goodness (see Rom. 7:12). We may also learn something of humanity's sinfulness (3:20; 7:7) and resultant temporal and eternal misery under the law's curse—that is, its threat or sentence of wrath against all transgressors (Deut. 27:26; Gal. 3:10). Furthermore, the law not only convinces people of their miserable sinfulness, it also teaches them their need of a savior. If we are to escape the law's rigorous demands, we need someone to meet those demands on our behalf—someone to render the obedience, someone to avert the penalty. Well, all this is most helpful, but we are left with the ultimate question: "O wretched man that I am! who shall deliver me from the body of this death?" (Rom. 7:24).

Thirdly, there is the all-important evangelical truth. The gospel, "the word of truth," discloses how sinners can be saved. Here we are taught the way back into the divine favor and blessing. God has loved this ruined world and given His Son to be a substitutionary Savior, so that believing sinners might be accounted righteous before Him, not on account of their merit, but through the blood and righteousness of Christ. "God sent forth his Son, made of a woman, made under the law, to redeem them that were under the law" (Gal. 4:4–5). Such is Christ's wonderful achievement, that there is eternal life laid up in heaven for all His people: a life far more excellent than this one, a life providing the ultimate spiritual experience, a life full to overflowing with blessedness, satisfaction, and enjoyment. "God hath given to us eternal life, and this life is in his Son" (1 John 5:11). In evangelical truth alone can rest be found for guilty, fearful, and despairing souls.

Observe that this is truth which emerges from a past eternity. James Durham once perceptively commented that the gospel is called "everlasting" (Rev. 14:6) on account of "the rise of it, from everlasting in God's plot and purpose."[3] It is nothing more nor less than the remedial part of the eternal decree.

Truth Originating in God

The truth originated in God. It is "the wisdom of God in a mystery, even the hidden wisdom, which God ordained before the world unto our glory" (1 Cor. 2:7; see also Eph. 3:9). The divine grace and mercy were responsible for it, as Paul made clear in his reference to God's "purpose and grace" (2 Tim. 1:9) and His "will" to show "mercy" (Rom. 9:15–16). "The gospel and all the truths of it have had the richest cabinet that ever there was. First it had God's heart, it was hid in God," wrote a Puritan.[4] This makes it the more wonderful. It arose in God. It came from the Everlasting. It was the product of infinite and amazing love: "God so loved the world…" (John 3:16).

Moreover, as an eternal purpose of love, this truth was framed by the three persons of the Holy Godhead, the Father, the Son, and the Holy Spirit. They simultaneously and unanimously agreed on the plan, which gave to it a definite covenantal form, "the everlasting [or eternal] covenant" (Heb. 13:20). Within the sacred enclosure of the Trinity, it was decided that an innumerable company of mankind should be redeemed from sin and misery, to holiness and happiness. The Son, who was designated as Redeemer (Isa. 42:1; 1 Peter 1:18–20), voluntarily and freely acquiesced in the arrangement,

---

3. James Durham, *Commentary on Revelation* (Glasgow: James Spencer, 1788), 593.

4. Goodwin, *Works*, 4:308.

saying, "I delight to do thy will" (Ps. 40:8; see also Isa. 40:10). Thus, the whole plan can be described as "the eternal purpose which he [God the Father] purposed in Christ Jesus our Lord" (Eph. 3:11). The eternal and blessed Spirit concurred with this, assuming the work of effectually applying redemption's benefits to elect souls. As a result, God's whole scheme is represented as "the mystery of his will, according to his good pleasure which he hath purposed in himself" (Eph. 1:9).

Christ, the Center of All Truth

The truth, then, is uniquely concentrated on the Son of God, our Lord Jesus Christ. It is "the mystery of Christ" (Col. 4:3). According to the first chapter of Ephesians, we are blessed with all spiritual blessings "in Christ," chosen "in him," predestinated to be adopted as children "by Jesus Christ," accepted "in the beloved," redeemed through blood in Him, gathered together in the fullness of time "in Christ," granted an inheritance in Him, brought to faith "in Christ," and sealed with the Holy Spirit of promise in Him (Eph. 1:3–14). Everything God has thought and planned is in Christ! The gospel concerns "the glory of God in the face of Jesus Christ" (2 Cor. 4:6). It states that "God was in Christ, reconciling the world unto himself" (5:19).

Back beyond all creation, in the depths of the divine essence, there was unimaginable and intense delight found in the person, office, and work of the Redeemer. As the one "set up from everlasting," Christ Himself said that He was ever with the Father and "daily his delight..." (Prov. 8:30; cf. Isa. 42:1). When, in the time appointed, He appeared on this earth, the Father looked with great complacency upon

His Son, saying, "This is my beloved Son, in whom I am well pleased" (Matt. 3:17).

The Son is also the object of supreme regard to the Holy Spirit, the third person of the Trinity, who found such pleasure in the Son that He joined with the Father in approval of His redeeming mission. This is clearly stated in Isaiah: "The Lord GOD, *and his Spirit*, hath sent me" (Isa. 48:16, emphasis added). During Christ's earthly ministry, He intimated on more than one occasion that the Spirit's thoughts were ever toward Him. "He shall testify of me" (John 15:26). "He shall glorify me: for he shall receive of mine, and shall shew it unto you" (16:14). Now, one so esteemed within the Godhead should be contemplated by us with profound respect and adoring wonder. In Christ Jesus, we are confronted with "the truth" (John 14:6; Eph. 4:21).

Furthermore, it must be said that Scripture puts tremendous emphasis upon the blood of Jesus Christ. Yet one would never know that from modern, contemporary preaching! So-called ministers subject their congregations to ethical or political discourses, and indeed, anything and everything but the authentic gospel of Christ. But what is that gospel? Its grand theme is the blood of Jesus Christ, which refers to our Lord's substitutionary work which involved the voluntary sacrifice of His life in the place of those He came to save.

Accordingly, believing souls previously in bondage to sin and its dreadful consequences are said to have "redemption through his blood" (Eph. 1:7). Formerly denied access to God, they now enjoy "boldness to enter into the holiest by the blood of Jesus" (Heb. 10:19). As Christ has atoned for their sins, there is "propitiation [that which appeaseth wrath]...in his blood" (Rom. 3:25). In fact, sinners are "justified by his blood" (Rom. 5:9). Here is the ground and source of their peace with God: Christ "made peace through the blood of his cross" (Col. 1:20). However defiled and unclean we are, "the blood of Jesus Christ his Son cleanseth us from all sin" (1 John 1:7). All comfort for troubled hearts proceeds from "the blood of sprinkling, that speaketh better things than that of Abel" (Heb. 12:24). William Reid was right when he said, "Atonement by the blood-shedding of Christ is the substratum of Christianity."[5] "Young man," said an old minister to one newly ordained, "preach the blood. There is no Gospel without the blood!"

Truth Concerning Life Everlasting

The truth also concerns eternal life. In the divine purpose this was an important objective (Acts 13:48). The inter-Trinitarian covenant (typified in the covenant made with Levi) was "a covenant...of life," even "eternal life," which God "promised" in Christ, our head and representative, "before the world began" (Mal. 2:5; Titus 1:2). This is therefore the sum and substance of the gospel testimony. It is that "God hath given to us eternal life, and this life is in his Son. He that hath the Son hath life" (1 John 5:11–12).

Ultimately, eternal life means the bestowal of all good and the removal of all evil. John beautifully described believers' state of blessedness in the book of Revelation: "God himself shall be with them, and be their God. And God shall wipe away all tears from their eyes" (Rev. 21:3–4). This will be our happy condition throughout the ages to come. In Joshua's time, God caused a day to be lengthened and the shadow on the sundial of Ahaz was made to move backwards, towards

---

5. William Reid, *The Blood of Jesus* (London: James Nisbet, 1865), 115.

the sunrise; but more wonderful by far will be that day, the beginning of which will be ever present and the end of which will never be known. Without interruption and without termination, we will live with God, *forever and forever.*

This is the truth which from before all time was "hid in God" and also "hid from ages and from generations" (Eph. 3:9; Col. 1:26). It excited the deepest interest of the holy angels. Philosophers made it the subject of their intense investigations. People in general sought an answer to the question of all questions, "What is truth?" Apart from special revelation given to God's own people, the truth was kept a safely guarded secret.

Truth Only from God

Why was the truth concealed? Surely, it was to show that only God knows the truth. Human beings cannot even begin to perceive it, let alone fully comprehend it. This realization is so very humbling. It makes every one of us wholly dependent upon divine grace. Moreover, the truth's rarity makes it extremely precious. It should therefore be valued above all other things. If we have never known it, we should diligently search the Scriptures where truth may be found. If, on the other hand, we have received the gift, it is incumbent upon us to discover its fullness and to live according to its excellence. Clear views of the truth bring amazement to our hearts and rejoicing to our lips. For so long it was withheld from the souls of men, yet it is our privilege to be instructed in this mystery of redemption. God has revealed to us what others longed to know. No wonder Christ said, "Blessed are your eyes, for they see: and your ears, for they hear" (Matt. 13:16). Somehow, the fact that the truth has been so carefully concealed makes its appearance the more wonderful. Paul could therefore speak of "the glorious gospel of the blessed God" (1 Tim. 1:11).

Since infinite glory redounds to God by the gospel scheme of salvation, He is determined to promote His revealed truth in all the world. Isaiah foretold that "out of Zion shall go forth the law, and the word of the LORD from Jerusalem" (Isa. 2:3). In literal accomplishment of that prediction, the Lord Jesus Christ commissioned the apostles to proclaim the truth "in Jerusalem, and in all Judaea, and in Samaria, and unto the uttermost part of the earth" (Acts 1:8; see also Luke 24:47).

It is by this means that our Lord asserts His authority. He rules by "the rod of" His "strength," which is none other than His Word (Ps. 110:2; Isa. 11:4). When the truth comes to sinners, it humbles them, convincing them of their guilty and wretched condition (Acts 2:37); yet that same truth makes known to them a savior, Christ, who is able, willing, and ready to save such as call upon Him (2 Cor. 4:4). Attended by the Holy Spirit, the truth brings sinners to give up their rebellion and to yield to Christ, to be saved by Him and also to serve Him. This is what David meant when he wrote, "Thine arrows are sharp in the heart of the king's enemies; whereby the people fall under thee" (Ps. 45:5). Paul used military imagery to make the point that although worldly weapons can kill the body, God's "weapons"—the doctrines of salvation—can accomplish something even more difficult, namely to bring to the point of surrender the opinions and purposes of human souls, "strong holds" such as unbelief, ignorance, and prejudice. Paul wrote that God's "weapons" are "mighty through God to the pulling down of strong holds...and bringing into captivity every thought to the obedience of Christ" (2 Cor. 10:4–5). Thus it is that sinners like Jannes and Jambres, who seemed determined to "resist the truth" (2 Tim. 3:8), were brought through faith to "the acknowledging of the truth which is after godliness" (Titus 1:1).

The Battle for Truth

It comes as no surprise to learn that Satan defiantly and resolutely opposes this truth. When Christ spoke of Satan's bitter antagonism, He declared that "from the beginning," Satan "abode not in the truth" (which appears to refer to the truth of the gospel) (John 8:44; see also vv. 31–32, 45–46). Did God give some intimation of His redeeming purpose to the newly created angels? Was their stubborn refusal to accept it the occasion of their tragic fall? This would seem to be what happened. But, be that as it may, it is an undeniable fact that throughout history Satan has consistently resisted the truth.

As Christ said, Satan is "a liar" and "the father of it" (John 8:44), which means that by his very nature he speaks nothing but lies. Satan, therefore, is responsible for the promotion of false religion in this world. Heathens worship their so-called "gods" at his instigation. Idolaters "offer their sacrifices unto devils" (Lev. 17:7; see also Deut. 32:17; 2 Chron. 11:15). Do some so-called Christians embrace a counterfeit form of Christianity? It is Satan who promotes false teaching. Scripture says that "some shall depart from the faith, giving heed to seducing spirits, and doctrines of devils" (1 Tim. 4:1; see also 2 Cor. 11:13–14; 2 Thess. 2:8–10). Satan, as the usurping "god of this world," spares no pains to propagate false religion. He does this on account of his bitter opposition to the truth.

Haters of Error

The Lord's people are distinguished by their love of the truth and hatred of error (Ps. 119:103–4; 2 Thess. 2:10). Enlightened by the Holy Spirit and instructed by the gospel, they esteem God's Word most highly, valuing it "better...than thousands of gold and silver"; hence, they meditate upon it day and night for their own spiritual comfort (Ps. 119:72, 52), and each of them "out of the good treasure of the heart bringeth forth good things" (Matt. 12:35), declaring and, if necessary, defending the truth of God. "For," writes the apostle, "we can do nothing against the truth, but for the truth" (2 Cor. 13:8).

What is the great cause we maintain? It is the cause of God and truth. Scripture speaks of the Christian church as "an army" (Song 6:10), and, in waging war against the enemy, the "banner" which must be raised and displayed is "the truth" (Ps. 60:4). Only the truth will destroy Satan's kingdom and, upon its ruins, establish the kingdom of God's Son. Only the truth will win sinners' hearts for the Savior. Only the truth will confirm believers in their faith. Hence, we set forth the truth, in such a way that it strikes home to the conscience and proves acceptable in the sight of an all-seeing and heart-searching God (see 2 Cor. 4:2).

Maintainers of All Truth

Moreover, it is the truth for which we contend—not an aspect of it, nor even the great essentials of it, but every single and precious doctrine of the truth. Luther declared that "rather heaven and earth should be blended together in confusion than one jot of truth perish."[6] This biblical truth is honored by bold, strenuous, and determined conflict, which alone explains exhortations such as these: "Watch ye, stand fast in

---

6. Luther, quoted by Thomas Manton, in *The Works of Thomas Manton* (London: James Nisbet, 1870), 4:316.

the faith, quit you like men, be strong" (1 Cor. 16:13); "Thou therefore endure hardness, as a good soldier of Jesus Christ" (2 Tim. 2:3); and "Earnestly contend for the faith which was once delivered unto the saints" (Jude 3).

In the early church, the apostles, preachers, and other leaders preached the Word. They did not use music, drama, mime, or any other wordly means. Their mandate was our Lord's Great Commission. They testified with the appointed instrument, and they saw souls wonderfully blessed through divine grace. Today, it is possible to be a popular communicator and to gather an impressive congregation, but if we resort to worldly methodology that entertains rather than instructs, there will be neither spiritual nor eternal benefits. Clever gimmickry never yet convicted souls of sin or converted them to Jesus Christ. It is *not* the way to pluck souls out of the flames.

What sad days we live in! Church buildings are undergoing radical change for the sake of orchestral music, theatrical display, and dance performance. Extra-biblical officers such as musical directors are becoming more prominent than ministers of the gospel. Some congregations prefer the arts to expository and applied preaching. Yet society desperately needs faithful verbal communication of the truth.

The famous Welsh preacher Martin Lloyd-Jones used the following illustration. Imagine a man, he said, who had suffered for years from a terrible and apparently terminal illness. Crippled and in extreme pain, he eventually learned of an eminent doctor who claimed to have found an effective cure. The sick man obtained an appointment. Treatment began at once, with dramatic results. He began to walk upright without pain. It was so wonderful! Life was once again worth living. One day, this happy man was walking down the street, and on the other side of the road, he saw someone who was evidently in his former condition. For a moment he looked at the stranger's twisted limbs and distorted face. Then, without a moment's further delay, he ran across the road to tell the poor man of the doctor and his cure. He urged him to visit the doctor at once, promising him that it would be the best thing he ever did.

The preacher observed that it was like that with the apostle Paul. When in his sinful misery, he had been introduced to the Savior, who gave him new life and peace. Later, around him he saw unsaved Jews and Gentiles afflicted with sin that ultimately would bring them to death and hell. He felt himself under the strongest obligation, born of gratitude and benevolence, to share the good news with sinners everywhere. "I am debtor," he wrote, "both to the Greeks, and to the Barbarians; both to the wise, and to the unwise" (Rom. 1:14).

Surely it would be ludicrous to offer music or mime to such a sufferer. We should speak to him of the one who is able to heal his progressive illness. Even so, the sinner needs to hear of Jesus Christ and His salvation. He needs to hear the truth!

The Responsibilities of Ministers
What, then, can ministers do to advance God's truth?

Ensure that they possess orthodox Christian faith. Paul clearly had doctrinal orthodoxy in mind when he referred to "holding fast the faithful word" (Titus 1:9). Those considering the ministry therefore need to come to grips with the doctrines rediscovered by the Reformers, who passed them on to us.

Preach and teach the grand truths from God's Holy Word.
They must not be "dumb dogs" that "cannot bark" (Isa. 56:10).
They must "open" the "mouth," and "speak...the things which
become sound doctrine" (2 Cor. 6:11; Titus 2:1). It is impossible
to overemphasize the importance of the ministry of preaching.
Preaching is a divine institution, appointed for the salvation
and edification of souls (Rom. 10:17; 1 Cor. 1:21). It is insepa-
rably linked to the gracious influence and ministry of the Holy
Spirit, who illuminates the mind, opens the heart, and turns
the will (Isa. 59:21; Acts 10:44; 1 Cor. 2:4). Ministers are not
called to entertain people by projecting themselves, displaying
their talents, or indulging in humorous or anecdotal addresses.
The apostolic injunction is to preach the word. The church desperately needs preachers, not comedians.

Proclaim all *biblical truth.* The apostle Paul stressed the
importance of declaring "all the counsel of God," by which he
meant the whole will or plan of God respecting the salvation of
sinners (Acts 20:27). Clearly, this will involve the preaching of
Jesus Christ: His glorious person (Zech. 13:7; John 10:31); His
everlasting love (Prov. 8:30–31; Hos. 2:19); His covenant engage-
ments (Ps. 40:6–8; Zech. 6:13); His self-disclosure in type and
prophecy (Acts 10:43; Col. 2:16–17); His appearance in human
flesh (John 1:14; Rom. 1:3); His satisfaction for the sins of His
people (Isa. 42:21; 53:8); His exaltation to inconceivable glory
(Mark 16:6, 19; Phil. 2:8–9); His ability and willingness to save
lost sinners (John 6:37; Heb. 7:25); His gracious and affectionate invitations (Matt. 11:28–30; Luke 14:16–23); His boundless
supply of spiritual benefits (John 1:16; Col. 2:10); and His
promise of glory in the world to come (Ps. 84:11; John 14:1–3).

This is only to mention some of the subjects. Jesus Christ, the Son of God, is an inexhaustible theme.

Proclaiming all biblical truth will involve addressing issues that may offend some: the absolute sovereignty of God, the total depravity of man, salvation by distinguishing and efficacious grace, the law as a rule of life for believers, and the judgment of the last great day. What is required is nothing more or less than the preaching of the whole Word of God.

Many years ago I lived in an old house in the south of England. In the 1950s it was renovated, and the workmen discovered between the floorboards a silver shilling dated 1603. We were all naturally excited by the find, but on closer examination, we discovered that the coin had been "trimmed." Apparently this was a common practice. Precious metal had been pared away from around the rim to be melted down for further gain. Of course, this had somewhat spoiled the coin. It had certainly diminished its value. However, a trimmed shilling is not half as bad as a trimmed gospel! Yet there are men in our pulpits who seem to excel in withholding certain revealed truths. A true and faithful minister will never do that. Like the prophet Micaiah, he will say, "As the LORD liveth, what the LORD saith unto me, that will I speak" (1 Kings 22:14).

Commit to lifelong study of the Word of God. Ministers should endeavor to become proficient in their particular discipline, the knowledge of God and the deep mysteries of the faith. There really is no excuse for ignorant ministers. God's Word tells them to "meditate" upon the revealed truths and to "give" themselves "wholly to them"—that is, to be completely absorbed in them—so that their "profiting may appear to all" (1 Tim. 4:15).

Preach to prevent corruption of the truth. Like Paul, ministers are "set for the defence of the gospel" (Phil. 1:17). Not only are they to "hold fast the form of sound words" (2 Tim. 1:13), but they are also "by sound doctrine both to exhort and to convince the gainsayers [critics]" (Titus 1:9). When false teaching arises, they must meet it head-on, wielding the sword of the Word of God. Of course, this might erode their popularity and support. Often we hear criticisms made of a faithful man: "He is becoming so negative. He always seems to be knocking things!" Well, friends, there is a time to knock things. If a venomous snake suddenly and menacingly comes your way, you would do well to deliver a crushing blow on its head. Heresy is more dangerous than any snake. It is able to destroy men's very souls for all eternity. Should ministers ignore heresy and hope it will not do too much damage? Shouldn't they strike it with the Scriptures of truth, and all the power at their disposal?

Spread the Word. Ministers must do everything in their power to ensure that people in this and in other lands hear Christ's saving gospel. In fulfilling the Great Commission, the apostles "ceased not to teach and preach Jesus Christ" (Acts 5:42). They "filled Jerusalem" with their "doctrine" (5:28) and, not content with that, they preached the gospel "in the regions beyond" (2 Cor. 10:16) and even "in all the world" (Col. 1:5–6; cf. v. 23).

Ministers cannot be idle; they have a duty to further the truth. Each day, around the world, some 420,000 people are born and about 160,000 die. Only the Lord Jesus Christ can save them. Knowing this, every minister should say with Paul, "Necessity is laid upon me; yea, woe is unto me, if I preach not the gospel!" (1 Cor. 9:16). Brethren, we should be far more evangelistic than we are, for "how shall they hear without a preacher?" (Rom. 10:14).

Live godly lives. A final responsibility of ministers is to exemplify the truth in godly and holy lives. They are bound to be "an example of the believers, in word, in conversation, in charity, in spirit, in faith, in purity" (1 Tim. 4:12; see also 1 Peter 5:3). Thus confirming and commending the truth, they will be able to direct precious souls to holiness and to heaven.

The Responsibilities of Members

Pray. Church members cannot preach, but they can pray. Paul urged the believers in Rome to "strive together" with him in their prayers (Rom. 15:30), and there are many other similar exhortations in his epistles (for example, Eph. 6:18–20; Col. 4:3; 1 Thess. 5:25). Do you regularly pray for your minister? Do you pray that, through his ministry, God will be pleased to bless and enlarge His kingdom, and establish the truth in hearts and in lives? You may not feel you can do very much, but you can certainly pray. There is no telling what God will do when He sets His people praying.

Witness. Whenever and wherever possible, believers also can bear witness to the Lord Jesus Christ. We are directed to "be ready always to give an answer to every man that asketh you a reason of the hope that is in you with meekness and fear" (1 Peter 3:15). How we should repent of guilty silence! Never be afraid to witness. Let the Word of God often pass from your lips. Tell friends and strangers alike of the truth they have never known, or long since forgotten. This is your way to lend support to the truth.

Live according to God's Word. God's Word provides a pattern for living. "The doctrine" is said to be "according to godliness": that is, it is designed to promote godliness (or God-likeness). When something of God is seen in us, others have to acknowledge the power of the truth. Instead of speaking against it, they will be brought to confess it (see Titus 2:5; 1 Peter 3:1).

Worship. Members can worship the Lord each Sabbath in His house, thereby supporting both the minister and the ministry. First, we must join and support a Reformed church where God is honored, believers are built up in their faith, and sinners are reached with the gospel of salvation. Once this is done we must prepare ourselves for worship each Lord's Day. It was a noble thing Cornelius said: "Now therefore are we all here present before God, to hear all things that are commanded thee of God" (Acts 10:33). What an encouragement that must have been to Peter! Perhaps it explains (at least in part) the power with which Peter preached on that occasion.

Do not be a spiritual gypsy! Once you find the truth, settle down under the teaching of it. By your regular attendance, strengthen the minister and the people who evidently believe and love God's Word. Just by being there at each service and meeting you can do something for the preservation of the truth.

Give. Members can give as the Lord prospers them. Christ requires support of His servants: "Even so hath the Lord ordained that they which preach the gospel should live of the gospel" (1 Cor. 9:14; see also Gal. 6:6; 1 Tim. 5:17–18). This is absolutely vital, of course, if the ministry of truth is to continue in a local church. Furthermore, since some of the money given will support others who are serving the Lord elsewhere

(Phil. 4:10–18), regular and generous giving is an excellent way to further the truth. It is significant that Scripture teaches us to contribute to the support of preachers "that we might be fellowhelpers to the truth" (3 John 6–8).

Exhort one another. Paul encouraged the Hebrews to "exhort one another daily" (Heb. 3:13). Mutual exhortation is a forgotten service. Yet each of us is his brother's keeper. If you see brothers or sisters beginning to doubt God's Word, and therefore faltering in the way of holiness, then go and speak to them, strengthening them in their most holy faith. That is what Jonathan did for David. He met with him in the wood and "strengthened his hand in God" (1 Sam. 23:16).

Encourage your ministers. Members generally should value, respect, and support their ministers. We should show godly love to them, and make it clear that we really do appreciate their ministry. The Galatians received Paul "as an angel of God, even as Christ Jesus" and he reminded them of this, telling them, "ye would have plucked out your own eyes, and have given them to me" (Gal. 4:14–15). It was not always thus (even with the Galatians), and, in sorrow, the apostle wrote to the Corinthian Christians, lamenting the fact that his love had not been reciprocated. "Our heart is enlarged," he said, "but ye are straitened in your own bowels"—that is, contracted or restricted in your affections (2 Cor. 6:11–12).

It can revive a minister's heart to hear how the Lord has been pleased to bless his preaching or visiting, but receiving little or no response from the congregation can cause a man to be terribly cast down. An encouraged minister can render exceptional service for Jesus Christ, but one discouraged finds it difficult to persevere. Surely, you want your minister to be valiant for the truth. Then, be sure to play your part. Support him all you can.

The Victory

What will happen to the truth? God's truth will ultimately triumph in this world. The truth will be victorious because God will not be robbed of His glory. He will have His perfections revealed and acknowledged. And this can only be as the nations come to know the gospel. "For from the rising of the sun even unto the going down of the same my name shall be great among the Gentiles" (Mal. 1:11). Accordingly, it is promised that in gospel times "the earth shall be full of the knowledge of the LORD, as the waters cover the sea" (Isa. 11:9; see also Hab. 2:14). The earth has not yet known such a blessing, and therefore we await the full accomplishment of this prophecy.

God will then hear the prayers of His people, prayers that have been offered from the commencement of this Christian era. What do believers pray for when they say, "Thy kingdom come"? They pray that God would send forth His servants, that the ministry of the gospel would be successful, and that the church would be so established in the earth that its kingdoms would become the kingdoms of the Lord and of His Christ. Such a prayer, expressing a desire that accords with the will of God, must one day be answered, to the blessing of men and women everywhere.

What if we do not see this yet? "For the vision is yet for an appointed time, but at the end it shall speak, and not lie: though it tarry, wait for it; because it will surely come, it will not tarry" (Hab. 2:3). The church's witness may seem to suffer loss, but a time of failure will be followed by a remarkable outburst of life and testimony (Rev. 11:11). Truth will not always be suppressed and despised: it is destined to rise again, with greater power and glory. In one of his letters, saintly Samuel Rutherford wrote to Marion M'Naught, a frequent correspondent: "I pray you comfort yourself in the Lord; for a just cause bides under the water only as long as wicked men hold their hand above it; their arm will weary, and then the just cause shall swim above, and the light that is sown for the righteous shall spring and grow up."[7]

We may rest assured from Scripture that when the enemy assails the truth (as at the present time), the Lord God Himself will interpose, exerting His divine power to preserve and advance the doctrine of the cross. "When the enemy shall come in like a flood, the Spirit of the LORD shall lift up a standard against him" (Isa. 59:19). May we not therefore hope for revival? Let the enemy do his worst; God will surely follow it with His best. That is why Christ once said, "I will build my church; and the gates of hell shall not prevail against it" (Matt. 16:18). He anticipated conflict, the conflict of the ages; but He declared that although all the schemes and powers of hell would be concentrated on the overthrow of the church, this would never prevail.

Far from suffering dreadful defeat, the church will remain unmoved in the evil day. It will survive the assault. It will prevail against its every foe. By virtue of the divine decree, Christ is destined to "reign"—until when?—"till he hath put all enemies under his feet" (1 Cor. 15:25). Among other things, this must surely mean that truth will finally triumph over error. The gospel will not prove weak, and fail. It will prove to be the power of God. Victory shall be with the truth! Anticipating that day, may we be more and more valiant for the truth!

---

7. Rutherford, *Letters*, 126–27.

Scripture Index